HARRIET TUBMAN

Other books by Judith Bentley

Busing: The Continuing Controversy
The Nuclear Freeze Movement

HARRIET TUBMAN

BY JUDITH BENTLEY

An Impact Biography
Franklin Watts
New York London Toronto Sydney 1990

Photographs courtesy of:
The New York Historical Society, NYC: pp. 14
(H. P. Moore), 99; The Bettmann Archive: pp. 20, 25, 31, 33, 43, 59,
96, 113; U.S. Library of Congress: pp. 36, 54, 72, 102, 110; Historical
Picture Society: p. 45; Kansas State Historical Society, Topeka: p. 85;
Chicago Historical Society: p. 99 inset; Culver Pictures: p. 121.

Library of Congress Cataloging-in-Publication Data

Bentley, Judith.
Harriet Tubman / by Judith Bentley.
p.   cm. — (An Impact biography)
Includes bibliographical references.
Summary: Details Harriet Tubman's life, experiences, and efforts
to aid slaves in escaping to the North, as well as her assistance to
the Union cause during the Civil War.
ISBN 0-531-10948-8
1. Tubman, Harriet, 1820?-1913—Juvenile literature. 2. Slaves-
-United States—Biography—Juvenile literature. 3. Afro-Americans-
-Biography—Juvenile literature. 4. Underground railroad—Juvenile
literature. 5. Slavery—United States—Anti-slavery movements-
-Juvenile literature. 6. Tubman, Harriet, 1820?-1913. [1. Slaves.
2. Afro-Americans—Biography.] I. Title
E444.T82B46 1990
305.5′67′092—dc20
[B]   [92]   90-12319   CIP   AC

CONTENTS

HARRIET TUBMAN

1

A NEGLECTED WEED

Harriet's mind was set on freedom. She had heard about places north and east of her Maryland plantation home where no one was a slave. She had heard that you could escape to freedom by following the Big Choptank River north; she knew that other slaves had made it. And she was thinking about going herself. In fact, she became set on it when she heard the rumor that she and her brothers would soon be sold south. The master had died, his widow needed cash, and a Georgia trader was in Bucktown, just a few miles away.

The year was 1849, and Harriet was about twenty-eight years old, living in a rural area on the Eastern Shore of Maryland on a plantation that grew corn and wheat and also raised slaves. Two of her older sisters had already been sold to a slave trader and led off in chains. She had seen them go—had watched from the top of a fence as one of them looked back at her children and wept. After that, Harriet had nightmares of horsemen coming and tearing shrieking women and children from each other. She wasn't about to let that happen to her.

She hated slavery, but the decision to run wasn't easy. Despite beatings and a blow to her head that was nearly fatal, Harriet's harsh childhood had been buffered by a large, loving family. Her husband was a free man. Because she was strong and hardworking, her master hired her out to others, and she was allowed to keep for herself a small amount of what she earned. Should she risk losing the few comforts she had for an escape attempt to a city of strangers? She decided for freedom, of course, but how did Harriet arrive at this moment when she knew she would run?

The story begins with a sassy young girl, the type who would tidy up the mistress's feather beds and then bounce on them in spite. She was a rebellious young member of the third generation of her family in America, one of 1,538,000 Afro-Americans living in slavery in the early nineteenth century.[1]

They had not always been slaves. Around the camp fires late in the evening, Harriet would have heard the old people talk about the kingdoms of Africa, where their people had lived for thousands of years until they were captured and traded to European merchants. She might have heard about the Fellata, known for their courage and love of freedom, or the Ashanti, a rebellious and heroic people who had fought off British invasions of their land. Both peoples had been among the four and a half million West African Negroes shipped in the 1700s from the Guinea coast, the area of Africa where a large chunk of land curves inward.

The old folks would tell of days chained below deck on slave ships without a glimpse of the sky, just the sickening pitch of the sea, of bodies so crowded together no one could move, of brackish water, and rotten food. Once here, they were sold on auction blocks as laborers for the tobacco fields in Virginia, Maryland, and the Carolinas. Their voices grieved over the land, the people, and the freedom they had lost.

Harriet's grandmother Modesty had come on one of those slave ships from Guinea and been sold to a family named Pattison in Dorchester County.[2] After fifty years in

America, her descendants had forgotten the words from their native African language that would have identified their tribal origin. Yet her granddaughter Harriet was always described as being "of pure African descent," with very dark skin and a "woolliness in her hair." From the way Harriet acted when she was young, people said she was "one of those Ashantis."[3]

It was not the old freedom in Africa that Harriet craved, however, but a new freedom from the drudgery and unease of the Brodess plantation. Her mother Rit had come to it in 1800 as a ten-year-old girl when her mistress, Mary Pattison, married Joseph Brodess. The Brodess brothers had cleared fertile fields on a 442-acre plot about 6 miles (9.6 km) east of the Chesapeake Bay near the hamlet of Bucktown. The slave cabins were set back from the main house, up against the edge of the Greenbriar Swamp. In one of those sagging cabins with buckling walls and a narrow, clay-daubed chimney, Harriet was born in 1820 or '21, a middle daughter of eleven children. She wasn't called *Harriet* at first because that was her mother's name—Harriet Green, or Rit for short. Instead she was named Araminta—Araminta Ross after her father Benjamin Ross—and called Minty.

"I grew up like a neglected weed," Harriet said of her childhood,

ignorant of liberty, having no experience of it. Then I was not happy or contented; every time I saw a white man I was afraid of being carried way. I had two sisters carried away in a chain gang—one of them left two children. We were always uneasy.[4]

At first, Rit was able to protect her daughter from the harsher experiences of slavery. Barefoot, wearing a coarse, scratchy shirt called a "Sally-go-naked shirt," Minty ran wild and chased rabbits. But this ended one day when a woman came driving up to the house looking for a girl to hire.

The woman wanted a girl—cheap—to take care of a baby and to do household chores. Since Minty was the youngest and thus cheapest slave, she was sent off in the lady's wagon without a word of explanation. Hardly bigger than the baby she took care of, Minty had to sit on the floor to hold it.

Rit hoped that her daughter would learn a domestic skill so that she would not have to work as a field hand, but her first job gave Minty a hatred of housework. The mistress ordered her to sweep and dust the parlor, but she didn't tell Minty how to do it. So Minty swept, and that went all right; then she dusted off the tables, chairs, and mantle. Soon the dust from the sweeping settled, and the chairs and tables were covered with dust again.

When the mistress came back and saw the dust, she grew angry at the frightened child and told her to do it again. So Minty did it again, and again—five times before breakfast—with the same result. The mistress resorted to the whip, and Minty screamed.

A visiting sister came into the parlor. "Why do you whip the child for not doing what she has never been taught to do?" The sister told Minty to open the windows and to sweep first. Then leave the room, she said, and set the kitchen table while the dust settled. Then come back and wipe the dust off. This worked, and there were no more beatings that day.[5]

Even after a long day of doing household chores, Minty was still expected to keep the baby from crying at night. She sat on the floor beside the cradle, rocking it continuously. If her head drooped, and her hand fell and the baby cried, the sleeping mother would awake and reach for the whip on a little shelf above her head. Minty never got enough sleep, and she was soon exhausted.

Perhaps she sang, to comfort herself and the baby: "Swing low, sweet chario-ot, coming fo' to carry me home." Perhaps she dreamed of a band of angels, coming to carry her home.

When Minty became nothing but skin and bones, the

mistress took her back to the Brodess home, reporting that "she wasn't worth sixpence." With love and herbal remedies, Rit nursed her daughter back to health, only to see her hired out again and again. From the time she was five or six, Minty knew the meaning of constant work, to the limits of her endurance.

Her family was a haven. Ben Ross was the supervisor of a timber crew that was foresting the land and hauling timber to the shipyards of Dorchester County and Baltimore. In 1840 he was listed in the census as a free black, but he came home at night to the slave cabin and his family. The Rosses were known to be "peculiarly intelligent, upright and religious people," with "a strong feeling of family affection."[6] By the 1820s and 1830s, the Brodess family fortunes were on the decline. Edward Brodess, son of Mary and Joseph Brodess, took over running the estate in 1824 when he married, but the farm did not flourish under his hands. He had nine children, and the main house began to look dilapidated.

At least some of his problems were economic. Maryland's tobacco had never been as high quality as Virginia's, and the crop had worn out the soil. Some slaveholders had already left to find fresh land; others had turned to growing crops such as corn, wheat, and rye, or fruits and vegetables. They still needed a large number of slaves who knew how to farm, but the slaves themselves became the most valuable "crop."

Brodess started selling slaves, especially women in their childbearing years, or hiring them out to other masters to bring in income. That's when Minty's two older sisters, Linah and Soph, were sold to the "new South"— Mississippi, Louisiana, and Alabama, where rice and cotton crops used up thousands of slaves each year in backbreaking work. Some of her brothers were hired out to nearby farms, and children such as Minty were hired out, too.[7]

Once Minty was sent to James Cook, whose wife was a weaver. Since cloth for a family or plantation was usually woven at home, this was a chance to learn a valued skill.

13

Slaves became valuable not only as
farm workers, but also as a commodity.

But Minty did not want to learn a house job, and Cook set her to watching his muskrat traps along the many streams and marshes in the Greenbriar Swamp. She felt sick and feverish one morning—it became measles—but Cook still sent her out to wade through the water and check the traps. When Rit heard that she had developed pneumonia, she asked Brodess to bring Minty back home, which he did, and Rit was able to nurse her back to health. Harriet later said that Brodess himself was never unnecessarily cruel but that some of those to whom she was hired out were tyrannical and brutal.[8]

Minty gained a reputation for being a bad child. Temptation overcame her once when she was taking care of a baby:

One morning, after breakfast [she] had the baby, and I stood by the table waiting until I was to take it; near me was a bowl of lumps of white sugar. My mistress got into a great quarrel with her husband; she had an awful temper, and she would scold and storm and call him all kinds of names. Now you know, I never had anything good, no sweet, no sugar; and that sugar, right by me, did look so nice, and my mistress's back was turned to me while she was fighting with her husband, so I just put my fingers in the sugar bowl to take one lump and maybe she heard me for she turned and saw me. The next minute she had the rawhide down. I gave one jump out of the door and I saw that they came after me, but I just flew and they didn't catch me. I ran and I ran and I passed many a house, but I didn't dare to stop for they all knew my mistress and they would send me back.

By and by when I was almost tuckered out, I came to a great big pig-pen. There was an old sow there, and perhaps eight or ten little pigs. I was too little to climb into it, but I tumbled over the high part and fell in on the ground; I was so beaten out that I could not stir.

15

*And there I stayed from Friday until the next
Tuesday, fighting with those little pigs for the po-
tato peelings and the other scraps that came down
in the trough. The old sow would push me away
when I tried to get her children's food, and I was
awfully afraid of her.*

*By Tuesday I was so starved I knew I had to go
back to my mistress. I didn't have anywhere else to
go, even though I knew what was coming. So I went
back.*[9]

Gradually, Minty learned ways of outwitting or evading her
mistresses to protect herself. When she realized that one
mistress usually whipped her in the mornings, she put on
extra layers of thick clothes when she dressed at the beginning of the day. If a whipping came her way, she just cried
loud and pretended she had been hurt; then, in the after-
noons, she would take off the heavy wrappings. Though she
was occasionally invited to join family prayers, she pre-
ferred to stay on the landing and pray for herself. "I prayed
to God to make me strong and able to fight."[10]

By all accounts she was a moody and willful child who
would fuss and sass people. Rit tried to shower affection
on Harriet when her rebellious ways got her into trouble,
but Rit worried aloud to Ben that their daughter was a
problem.

One way to deal with a difficult child was religion. Ben
and Rit were regular churchgoers—there was a slave church
down a path through the woods—and Minty learned Bible
verses. Her favorite was "Lo', I am with you always, even
unto the end of the world." She also liked the Bible verses
about deliverance. If she heard of a fugitive on his way
north, she thought of the verse "Hide the outcast; betray
him not that wandereth."

Spirituals, too, were a comfort. Minty had nightmares
about screaming women and children being torn apart by
men on horseback, but sometimes she had dreams of flying
through the air, over fields and rivers until she reached a

16

line. On the other side of the line were beautiful ladies in white stretching out their arms to her—"a band of angels waiting there for me."

Around those same camp fires where the old folks told stories of Africa, others sang songs that promised a new freedom, songs that used biblical themes to describe the experiences of slaves in America. As they sang, the grieving turned to yearning for a freedom regained:

> Didn't my Lord deliver Daniel,
> deliver Daniel, deliver Daniel?
> Didn't my Lord deliver Daniel,
> Then why not every man?

As Minty grew older, religion and rebellion seemed to war within her. Rebellion would lead her into trouble, but religion would provide a way out.

2

REBELLION

The young Araminta Ross was not the only slave with rebellion on her mind. She had grown up hearing whispered
accounts of slave revolts. In her grandmother's time, white
refugees had streamed into Baltimore fleeing from a bloody
slave uprising in Haiti, where a black republic was successfully established. In the United States, Gabriel Prosser had
planned a night attack on Richmond, Virginia, with a force
of more than a thousand blacks, but he failed. Around the
time Minty was born, Denmark Vesey recruited thousands
of supporters in a plan to kill the whites in Charleston,
South Carolina, but he was betrayed and hanged. Word of
such revolts had caused the town of Cambridge, twelve
miles to the north of Minty's home, to appoint a constable
"as the peace of the town was much disturbed by frequent
meetings of Negroes."[1]

The peace of the area was further threatened in the
spring of 1831, when Minty was about eleven years old.
There were reports of disorderly conduct in southeastern
Maryland and other coastal states, caused by the presence of
dealers who were buying slaves and selling them south.
Then, in August, disorder erupted in neighboring Virginia

when a slave named Nat Turner led a band of black men in killing fifty-seven white men, women, and children.

Nat Turner was an intelligent young man who brooded about slavery. His mother had told him that he was born to deliver his people from bondage, just as Moses had led the Hebrew people out of Egypt. She sang songs to him and repeated parts of biblical prophecy. When Nat learned to read, he devoured the Old Testament, which he thought justified war against evil. The same spirit that spoke to the prophets spoke to him, he said.

The eclipse of the sun in February had been a sign to him that the time for revolt had come. "I was told I should arise and prepare myself and slay my enemies with their own weapons," Turner said.[2] By preaching and exhorting at slave gatherings, Turner persuaded seventy others to join the revolt. They began late on a Sunday night, slaying Turner's master and his family in their bedrooms, and continued through the night and next day, killing every white person they found. It took three U.S. Army regiments to stop them, and Nat eluded pursuers for two months before he was arrested and hanged in November.

Word of the rebellion and pursuit spread quickly north from Virginia, from plantation to plantation and through the towns, where blacks who could read relayed the newspaper dispatches. Minty heard about Prophet Nat when the reports and rumors reached the general store at Bucktown, the crossroads two miles from the Brodess plantation. To slaveholders, the news was a nightmare come to life. But blacks were frightened, too, for they were more likely to suffer the consequences of the slaveholders' fear. Indeed, the lower parts of the Eastern Shore peninsula were "much agitated by apprehensions of a servile insurrection, and a good many persons of color were arrested—many expresses sent off for arms and men, and awful reports were heaped upon one another by fear!"[3] In areas where whites did retaliate, fifty-five blacks were killed without a trial.

To slaves on the Eastern Shore, Turner's revolt demonstrated how futile resisting slavery could be and how

This woodcut shows the capture of Nat Turner two months after he led a slave rebellion in 1831.

harsh the response, but the dream of deliverance lived on. Not just in Bucktown, but all over the South, slaves believed that a Moses would arise to lead them.

Minty, too, heard the dream. When slaves gathered from several plantations she learned the song of rebellion, "Go Down, Moses." A leader would sing the first line in each stanza—"When Israel was in Egypt land"—and the people would respond: "Let my people go." The leader would sing another line—"Oppressed so hard they could not stand"—with the response: "Let my people go." Then all would join in the chorus:

> Go down, Moses, way down in Egypt land
> Tell Ol' Pharaoh, to let my people go.

Because the message in the song was so obvious, the slaves were forbidden to sing it. Religious gatherings of blacks were also forbidden, unless they were led by a white minister, and it became illegal for anyone to teach a black to read or write. Araminta remained illiterate all of her life, but she grew up with the words of the song in her head and the promise in her heart.

On the Brodess plantation and the nearby Ross, Hughes, and Meredith farms, life went on amid heightened tension between the races. The work pace followed the seasons, with the need for slave labor greatest at harvest time. Fall days meant long hours of work into the evening, cleaning up the wheat or husking the corn. Too uncooperative to be a house slave, Minty had convinced Brodess to let her work in the fields. At the age of nine, she was hired out to a farmer for whom she did chores like hauling wood and splitting rails.

As she entered her teen years, the name Araminta or Minty was replaced by the common slave name Harriet, or Hatt, for short, although Harriet insisted that God always addressed her as Araminta. She was only five feet tall and quite ordinary looking, with short, crinkly hair, eyes that were becoming sullen and heavy-lidded, and a protruding lower lip. Working outdoors, she developed strong muscles, broad shoulders, and calloused hands. Her only clothes were long flax shirts that reached to her knees and were tied around the waist.

Older field hands taught her not only how to hoe a straight row but also folk history, superstitions, and songs. Slaves working in the fields may have seemed content to the overseer, especially when they were singing; the songs, however, had hidden meanings. They were full of chariots, trains, ships, rivers, the sea, and the promised land, all code words for talking about escaping. Harriet sang often, especially in the fields. Sometimes she composed her own verses to familiar songs. By paying attention to slaves' reactions to the overseer, she became alert to the undertones of their words.

Hatt learned too fast. She gained a reputation among the field hands as a young spitfire who dared to laugh out loud at the overseers. One overseer in particular was greatly feared by the slaves, who would go out of their way to avoid walking past him. Harriet seemed to have more curiosity than fear.

Hatt was working late one evening, husking corn, when a young slave named Jim who belonged to a farmer named Barrett began "looking mighty greasy," meaning that he might be planning to slip away. Soon he did leave his post, without asking permission of the overseer. As he headed down the road toward the Bucktown store, the overseer followed. Hatt left, too, cutting across the fields to get a head start.

When the overseer caught up with Jim at the store, he swore he would whip the fugitive and called on Harriet to help tie him up. Harriet refused to move, and Jim began edging toward the door. As he made a dash through it, Harriet blocked the overseer's way. Enraged, the man grabbed a two-pound weight from the scale on the counter and hurled it after the fleeing slave. Instead of hitting Jim, the weight hit Harriet, right in the middle of her forehead, and she slumped heavily to the floor.[4]

Seemingly lifeless, Hatt was carried the two miles home to her mother's cabin. No one thought she would live. For days, she lay unconscious on a bundle of rags on the floor of the cabin. The lead weight had pushed a portion of her skull against her brain and left a dent in her forehead for the rest of her life.

Rit treated the wound as best she could with loving care and home remedies. All fall of that year (probably 1835), Harriet was sick and disabled; she lost weight, slept much of the time, and cried out in pain.

Master Brodess occasionally looked in on the unconscious child to see whether she was recovering. He was hoping to sell her. As soon as she came to, he brought in prospective buyers, even though she was much diminished in value.

"All the time he was bringing men to look at me, and they stood there saying what they would give and what they would take," Harriet recalled years later. "They wouldn't give a sixpence for me."

By Christmas, Harriet was able to get up, to move around a little, and to come out of the cabin. Believing that God was with her in recovery, she began to pray fervently as she did a few chores.

'Pears like, I prayed all the time, about my work, everywhere, I was always talking to the Lord. When I went to the horse-trough to wash my face, and took up the water in my hands, I said, "Oh, Lord, wash me, make me clean." When I took up the towel to wipe my face and hands, I cried, "Oh Lord, for Jesus' sake, wipe away all my sins!"

Besides praying away any sins of her own, Harriet also began praying about slavery, for a change in people's hearts. She prayed especially hard when the master was trying to sell her: " 'Oh Lord, convert ole master; change that man's heart!' "

The fear of revolts like Turner's had forced Southerners

23

to look at the problem in their midst. A few Marylanders, mainly from Baltimore, had even suggested that slavery be abolished in the state, but it was not seriously considered. Others suggested that freeing a slave be conditioned on the freed person leaving the state, but farmers needed the labor of free blacks, so they opposed that idea. The Maryland General Assembly promoted colonization, encouraging freed blacks to move to Liberia, a colony in Africa, but to most Afro-Americans, the offer seemed like a swindle, a way to be sent away from the country of their birth. Ultimately the citizens of Maryland were unable to find a satisfactory solution.

So there came a time when Harriet gave up on converting old master from his dependence on slavery. She heard through the slave grapevine that, as soon as she recovered, she was to be sent with her brothers on the chain gang to the far South. She changed her prayer. "When I took up the broom and began to sweep, I groaned 'Oh Lord, whatever sin there be in my heart, sweep it out Lord, clear and clean, but I can't pray no more for poor old master. Lord, if you ain't never going to change that man's heart kill him Lord, and take him out of the way, so he won't do more mischief.' "

Later, the master did die, and Harriet, believing in the power of prayer, regretted her thoughts.

Then it appeared like I would give the world full of silver and gold if I had it, to bring that poor soul back, I would give myself; I would give everything! But he was gone, I couldn't pray for him no more.[5]

The mark on Harriet's forehead remained a visible scar of the brutality of slavery. The wound went deep into her heart. Earl Conrad, who has written the most comprehensive biography of Harriet Tubman, argued in a letter to a descendant, "That fellow who hit her over the head when she was about fifteen was the nearest thing to god that she ever got; that was her baptism, and her blessing."[6]

A photograph of a relief of
Harriet Tubman as a young woman

After her recovery her eyes remained dull, but her mind was always busy, thinking about slavery. The blow revealed the fullness of the mean-spirited system that oppressed her and its inability to change. It deepened her resolve not to accept slavery as her lot in life. If masters would not end slavery, she would act to free herself. For the next few years, however, she bided her time.

3
HALF SLAVE, HALF FREE

When Harriet went back to work in the fields in the spring of 1836, the white people on the plantation thought she was half-crazy, or at least half-witted, as a result of the injury. When owners came near, she kept quiet. To them she seemed useless and damaged because she was too clever to show the thoughts that were going through her mind.

Several times a day, the pressure on her brain caused her to fall asleep suddenly, no matter what she was doing—standing up, clinging to a gatepost, sitting on a fence. "Look at Hatt, she's done gone off again," onlookers would say. Just as abruptly as she had fallen asleep, she would awaken and begin doing again whatever she had been doing. She also staggered sometimes as she walked, but her mind was steady.

As she recovered her strength, Hatt began to fill out, but she was not a pretty girl. To be unattractive was actually a blessing to a young slave entering her childbearing years. A plain woman could avoid catching the eye of the master or the overseer and thus be spared unwanted attention.

In her teens Hatt graduated from wearing coarse shirts to wearing cast-off dresses. A colorful bandanna protected

27

her head from the sun. She wore her bandanna like a badge—a sign of her courage and the spirit that had brought her through times of trouble.

Although Edward Brodess inherited the slaves on the plantation, his stepbrother, Dr. Anthony Thompson, was their supervisor. Doc Thompson was a "spare-built man" who covered his bald head with a wig and stinted on food and clothing for his slaves.[1] He was not a medical doctor, as his title implies, but a preacher of sorts who also dabbled in real estate.

Since Brodess couldn't find a buyer for her, Harriet persuaded Thompson to allow her to "hire out" her time, which meant working for other farmers while giving most of what she earned to her master. Despite that obligation, hiring out was one way for a slave to gain some slight independence and even money of his or her own.

Harriet's father, Ben Ross, had become a valued employee of a shipbuilder and timber operator named John Stewart. In the mid-1800s, shipbuilding was a growing business in Dorchester County, as well as in Baltimore, up Chesapeake Bay. Vast quantities of oak and pine trees were cut down in the country, providing a good source of income to the landowners. Harriet's father was the inspector for one of Stewart's lumbering crews, supervising the cutting and hauling of the wood.

Harriet began hiring out to John Stewart soon after her head injury. At first she worked in the house, but then she worked in the open fields, doing the hardest jobs, like driving oxen and plowing, sometimes cutting wood and hauling logs with her father. She may have chosen outdoor work as a way to remain active and keep her blood circulating in hopes that this would counteract the sleeping spells. Stewart was a more lenient man than her other masters had been, and she worked for him steadily for five or six years.

Doing the work of a physical laborer, Harriet grew strong. "I could tote a flour barrel on one shoulder," she later bragged.[2] Her father was known as a superior workman and could earn as much as $5 a day. A man who hired his time was expected to earn $100 to $150 a year for his master, a woman $50 or $60. By cutting a half cord of wood a day, Harriet earned enough money beyond what she owed her master to buy herself a pair of oxen worth $40.

Sixty years later stories describing Harriet's strength exaggerated it greatly. A reporter who interviewed her for the *New York Herald* said that

before she was nineteen years old, she was a match for the strongest man on the plantation of the new master to whom she now belonged. He would often exhibit her feats of strength to his friends as one of the sights of his place. She could lift huge barrels of produce and draw a loaded stone boat like an ox.[3]

Descendants of her relatives say, however, that she should not be compared to an ox,[4] that her strength was more mental than physical, developing over the years from courage, patience, and wisdom.

Working for Stewart broadened Harriet's acquaintance with the community of slaves who worked the farms around Bucktown and cut down the timber around Cambridge in the 1830s and 1840s. From them she heard that many slaves were escaping from Dorchester County by way of a mysterious *underground railroad,* a linkage of people who would help a slave make a break for freedom. If you could find a *station* on the railroad, the *agents* would give you food, shelter, and sometimes a ride to the next stop.

The success of the runaways and the underground railroad caused angry talk among Dorchester slaveholders who complained about the *abolitionists* in the North. Slave owners talked about *the fruit of abolition* whenever a slave killed his master, set fire to a barn, or ran away. Frederick Douglass, who was also a slave on the Eastern Shore, heard about abolitionists before he escaped in 1838, but he didn't know what the word meant. Since he could read, he looked up the word *abolition* in the dictionary. ''The act of abolishing,'' it said, but what, he wondered, were they trying to abolish? Finally, he read in a newspaper about petitions for the abolition of slavery in the District of Columbia, and he understood.[5]

The movement to abolish slavery began early in American history, particularly among certain religious groups, including the Quakers (also called Friends). The Philadelphia Yearly Meeting of Friends decided in 1776, as the American Revolution began, that no Quaker members in and around Philadelphia could continue to hold slaves.

After the Revolution, the liberating spirit grew stronger. One by one, Northern states proclaimed the abolition of slavery within their borders, beginning with Vermont in 1777, then Massachusetts and Pennsylvania in 1780. In Maryland, too, a signer of the Declaration of Independence—Charles Carroll—introduced a bill in the state senate aimed at gradually abolishing slavery, but the bill failed. A committee of the Maryland Assembly said in 1827 that it recognized slavery as a "grievous national calamity," but that it could not follow the Northern example of freeing slaves: "With them the evil to be subdued was a pigmy, with us it is a monster."[6]

Impatient at the Southern response to the "monster," a young editor in Baltimore named William Lloyd Garrison called for immediate emancipation, or freeing, of all slaves. Garrison declared that holding slaves any longer was tyrannical and that slavery was an agreement with Hell, a comparison Harriet would make later when she spoke out in the North.

Talk of immediate emancipation alarmed slaveholders on the Eastern Shore. After Nat Turner's revolt, it sounded downright dangerous. Who were these meddlers endangering the lives of Southern whites by encouraging slaves to take freedom into their own hands? The Maryland legislature set a ten- to twenty-year jail term for anyone preparing printed or written material "having a tendency to create discontent among the colored people or to stir them to insurrection."

Field hands seldom knew how to read, however, and few abolitionist tracts reached them. What did reach them were whispers about slaves who had run and the names of

This painting depicts a convention of the Anti-Slavery Society in 1840.

people who might help. Often no one knew if a fugitive had made it. Some were caught, returned to their masters, severely flogged, and sent farther south. Some turned up buried in the backyard of a notorious Eastern Shore slave catcher named Patty Cannon. Cannon captured fugitives and free blacks alike and sold them back into slavery. She was convicted of murder and died in jail in 1829, but the fear of slave catchers and ''patterrollers'' on the roads lived on. Even as Harriet heard about freedom, she knew it would not be easy.

A slave woman who could earn enough money to buy herself a pair of oxen attracted some attention around Bucktown, especially from a free black man named John Tubman who worked odd jobs on the farms and plantations of the area in the early 1840s. Tubman was the son of slaves who had served a wealthy, landowning family, the Tubmans, from whom they had taken their last name. The original settler, Justice Richard Tubman, had moved to Dorchester County in 1669 and received about a thousand acres of land for his military service against the Indians. The Tubman slaves—John Tubman's parents, grandparents, and perhaps his great-grandparents—had served in the family's mansion, at the western edge of Cambridge on the Choptank River. John's parents had been freed by the Tubmans, so he was free, too.

Free blacks were not uncommon in Dorchester County. Of the approximately 8,200 blacks living there in 1840, almost half were freed, and their number was increasing. Together, the number of slaves and free blacks was approaching the number of whites. Although their labor was needed, free blacks were regarded with some alarm; they were seen as a nuisance, as troublemakers, a source of cheap labor, and competition for jobs. They were also seen as ''a curse to our slaves, whom they are constantly corrupting.''[7]

Then in her early twenties, Harriet was in the mood for a little ''corrupting.'' She was too old to remain unmarried much longer; slave girls almost always married in their teens. Normally a master chose a mate for his female slaves

EMANCIPATOR—*EXTRA.*

NEW-YORK, SEPTEMBER 2, 1839.

American Anti-Slavery Almanac for 1840.

The seven cuts following, are selected from thirteen, which may be found in the Anti-Slavery Almanac for 1840. They represent well-authenticated facts, and illustrate in various ways, the cruelties daily inflicted upon three millions of native born Americans, by their fellow-countrymen! A brief explanation follows each cut.

The peculiar "Domestic Institutions of our Southern brethren."

Selling a Mother from her Child.

Mothers with young Children at work in the field.

A Woman chained to a Girl, and a Man in irons at work in the field.

"They can't take care of themselves"; explained in an interesting article.

Hunting Slaves with dogs and guns. A Slave drowned by the dogs.

Servility of the Northern States in arresting and returning fugitive Slaves.

The Emancipator *was an antislavery newspaper.*

with an eye to producing strong children, but Harriet had been able to put this off, perhaps because of her injury, her dull appearance, and her value as a laborer.

Some say Harriet was attracted to John Tubman because he was a free spirit, working when and where he could. Others say she married him because he was literate or that her mother forced the marriage.[8] Whatever the explanation, Harriet and John were united in 1844 or 1845 and lived together for the next five years. Allowing a slave to marry a free black was a bit unusual, and the marriage was a slight improvement in social status for Harriet.

It also gave her a closer look at freedom. She was always asking John about his freedom. Why and how had his parents been manumitted, she wanted to know. Many slaves were freed "for conscience' sake," according to Frederick Douglass. Some were freed as a reward for their loyalty and hard work. A landowner's will frequently stipulated that his slaves were to receive their freedom after a certain number of years of service to the new owner. They could not be freed, however, just to relieve their owners of an economic burden when they became old. The first Maryland law on manumission, in 1752, said that slaves to be freed had to be sound in body and mind, capable of labor, and not over fifty.

If a master would not give freedom, some slaves purchased it. Neither path seemed open to Harriet. Pay for hired workers was so low that self-purchase was not easy. At forty dollars a year in earnings above what she paid her master, it would take Harriet twenty-five years to buy her freedom. She would be almost fifty before she could earn enough.

There must be another way. Maybe Rit planted a question in Harriet's mind because soon after her marriage to John Tubman, Harriet decided to check on Athon Pattison's will, the will that had given Modesty's little girl Rittia to his granddaughter Mary Pattison. "I paid a lawyer $5 to look up the will of my mother's first master," Harriet recounted. "He looked back sixty years and said it was time to give up.

34

I told him to go back farther. He went back sixty-five years, and there he found the will."[9]

"I give and bequeath unto my granddaughter, Mary Pattison," the will read, "one Negro girl called 'Rittia' and her increase until she and they arrive to forty-five years of age."

"Rittia and her increase"—that was Harriet and her brothers and sisters—until she and they were forty-five. What did it mean? It sounded like Rit should have been freed when she reached forty-five, which was about 1835. Any of her children born after that (there may have been one) would be free, too. Children born before that (like Harriet) would also be free when they reached forty-five.

Although the legal implications of the will are not that clear, Harriet thought her mother had been wrongfully kept in slavery. She mistakenly thought that Mary Pattison had died soon after the will was made and that Rit should have been freed then. Mary Pattison did not die young, however, but married Joseph Brodess. Her slave Rittia passed to her son Edward, with whom Harriet was stuck, at least until she turned forty-five. Nothing came from looking up the will.

After a few years of hiring her time to John Stewart, Harriet went back to working under the supervision of Doc Thompson from 1847 to 1849, an experience she must have found hard to bear. Besides "pretending to preach," as Rit and Ben described it, Thompson dealt in slaves and real estate. Thompson had owned many slaves and a dozen farms at one time, they said, but "in consequence of having reached out too far, several of his farms had slipped out of his hands," and circumstances forced him to make frequent sales of slaves.[10]

That made Harriet uneasy. She was married to a free man, earning some money of her own, working in fields she knew, and surrounded by a family she loved, but she was not satisfied to be half-free. The old nightmares continued to haunt her, particularly the one of horsemen coming in the night. She was afraid of being sold.

Harriet said she felt a divine presence always near her,

*Frederick Douglass was a friend
and ally of Harriet Tubman.*

and during this period of her life, she began to experience visions. "We'd been carting manure all day, and t'other girl and I were gwine home on the sides of the cart," Harriet related, "and another boy was driving, when suddenly I heard such music as filled all the air," and saw a vision.[11] Harriet believed she inherited visionary power from her father, who could always predict the weather and who foretold the Mexican War before it started in 1846.

Her escape dream of flying over a line dividing the land of slavery from the land of freedom also recurred. Flying over green fields, towns, rivers, and mountains like a bird, she would reach a fence or sometimes a river, "but it 'peared like I wouldn't have the strength." Just as she was sinking down, ladies dressed in white would be reaching out to her. Often she got stuck in a quagmire or the ground buckled underneath her in the dream; sometimes the women pulled her across.

Always in her visions were voices beckoning to her. "Come. Arise. Flee for your life," they warned.[12]

John made light of her fears and her dreams. He seemed unconcerned about her status as a slave and decidedly uninterested when she talked of going north. They must have been a contrasting pair —he unworried, easygoing, content; she moody, intense, dissatisfied.

What makes a slave decide to make the break for freedom? Frederick Douglass wrote of his own indecision before he decided to flee: "the wretchedness of slavery and the blessedness of freedom were perpetually before me." Fears of starvation and pursuit sometimes made him "rather bear those ills we had, than fly to others, that we knew not of. . . . At times we were almost disposed to give up, and try to content ourselves with our wretched lot. At others, we were firm and unbending in our determination to go."[13]

It was the fear of being sold that finally made Harriet, too, firm and unbending in her decision to flee.

4
ESCAPE

Edward Brodess died on March 9, 1849, and rumors swept through the slave quarters. The master's will gave all his property, including the slaves, to his widow Elizabeth, or Eliza Ann. Sale of slaves could bring ready cash to the widow, who might not want to continue farming on her own.[1]

Harriet worried about herself and her family. Ben was free, and Rit was too old to be sold, but Harriet and several of her brothers and sisters were prime workers and would fetch a good price. Although they were still under the supervision of Doc Thompson, Eliza Ann would make the decisions about their future.

The general anxiety abated when the word came that none of the slaves was to be sold out of state. Harriet relaxed for a time, but the voices telling her to flee did not subside. Then, in the summer, information came from a slave on another plantation: The Georgia trader was in Bucktown, and Harriet and her brothers would be sold and sent south with a gang bought up for plantation work.

Suddenly the choice between running and staying was clear. "There are two things I've got a right to," Harriet

38

vowed, "and these are death or liberty. One or the other I mean to have."[2]

The risks of running were high. Maryland laws favored the property rights of slave owners over the human rights of a slave. Trying to escape was a felony, punishable by whipping, cropping (cutting off of the ears), or branding. A runaway who was caught would be held in jail until claimed by the owner or sold out of state, if unclaimed.

Helping a runaway was also a risk. The year Brodess died, the maximum jail term for anyone encouraging or helping a slave to run away was increased from five to fifteen years. The helper was also required to pay the owner the full value of the slave, usually about a thousand dollars.

Those who caught runaways were rewarded with cash. Patrols of local white men reinforced the sheriff when there were rumors of runaways, and they would be paid for delivering a fugitive to a justice of the peace. There was no punishment at all for anyone who "should chance to kill a runaway slave forcibly resisting capture."[3]

In spite of these odds, 279 slaves would run away from their owners in Maryland in 1849, not including runaways from Dorchester County. Harriet was determined to add to the number. "No one will take me back alive," she promised herself. "I shall fight for my liberty, and when the time has come for me to go, the Lord will let them kill me."[4]

Slaves who were courageous enough to take a chance and run were often the misfits on a plantation. Like Harriet, many had enjoyed near freedom as hired workers; they were self-reliant, highly intelligent, and aware of the world beyond slavery. When they heard rumors of sale to the deep South, they knew what they could expect.

Of the North, however, they knew very little, except the cold winters their masters had told them about. Slaves in states that bordered on free states at least knew that such states existed, but they had only a vague idea of geography and no access to maps. The distance from Dorchester County to Philadelphia was only a hundred miles for a crow but closer to two hundred miles for a person. Traveling on

39

foot through completely unfamiliar terrain, it would take at least a week and probably more.

Harriet was certain of a few things. She knew that freedom lay to the north, that the Big Choptank River, the largest river on the Eastern Shore, flowed from the northeast, that the North Star would guide her on a clear night, and that moss grows thicker on the north side of trees. Years of working outdoors, learning from her father, and talking to slaves and free blacks such as John Tubman had broadened her knowledge of areas beyond Bucktown and the Brodess plantation. She had a gift for geography and an unerring memory of places she had been. Although she was completely illiterate, not even knowing which side of a book was up, Harriet was a clever, self-reliant woman.

Knowing that Ben and Rit would be questioned when she was found missing, Harriet did not want to put them in greater jeopardy by telling them her intentions. She did not want them to worry, however, that she had been sold. Since her husband was unsympathetic to her plans, she tried to tell her niece Mary Ann, who was working in the kitchen of the big house. Because there were too many people around, Harriet engaged in some roughhouse to draw Mary Ann away from the house. Before they could talk, however, the master came riding up on horseback, and Mary Ann went back in.[5]

Frustrated in her efforts, and with little time to spare, Harriet resorted to a common way slaves had of communicating forbidden thoughts. She burst into song:

> When that ol' chariot comes,
>   I'm going to leave you,
> I'm bound for the promised land,
>   Friends I'm going to leave you.
>
> I'm sorry I'm going to leave you,
>   Farewell, oh farewell;
> But I'll meet you in the morning,
>   Farewell, oh farewell.

40

I'll meet you in the morning,
    I'm bound for the promised land,
On the other side of Jordan,
    Bound for the promised land.

The tune was probably an old Methodist one, but Harriet
made up her own words for the occasion, drawing from the
images of her religious experience. The Jordan River was
the Mason-Dixon line, separating slave states from free
states; the other side, the promised land, was the North.
Harriet herself was later called "ole Chariot" for all the
traveling and rescuing she did.

The spiritual "Steal Away" was also commonly used
as a code:

Steal away, steal away,
Steal away to Jesus!
Steal away, steal away home,
I ain't got long to stay here.

My Lord, He calls me,
He calls me by the thunder,
The trumpet sounds inna my soul,
I ain't got long to stay here.

When it was dark, Harriet stole away to the east, following
the Greenbriar Swamp along the edge of the Brodess fields
to the hamlet of Bucktown. The first time Harriet escaped
she started out with three of her brothers, but they developed cold feet. Fearing recapture, they persuaded Harriet to
go back. She lay low for a day and then started east again.[6]

From years of secretiveness, necessary for her self-
preservation, Harriet never described her own escape route
or the names of people in Maryland who helped her. More
is known about her later trips to rescue others than is known
about the first one. It is thought, however, that she began
with the aid of a white Quaker woman in Bucktown. There
is some indication that Harriet had known this woman for

several years and that the woman had promised her aid in case she ever decided to run.

The account comes from a later neighbor of Harriet's, Helen W. Tatlock. "The white woman gave her a paper with two names upon it," Mrs. Tatlock recounted, "and directions how she might get to the first house where she would receive aid."

> *Harriet had a bed quilt, which she highly prized, a quilt she had pieced together. She did not dare to give this to any of the slaves, for if this was found in their possession, they would be questioned and punished for having known about her plans. She gave this bed quilt to the white woman.*"[7]

Leaving the fields and woods around Bucktown, Harriet reached the first house the woman had directed her to. When she arrived and showed the woman of the house the paper, she was told to take a broom and sweep the yard. This may have surprised her, but she asked no questions. She might have guessed that a black woman doing chores was a good disguise for nosy neighbors.

The woman's husband, who was a farmer, came home in the early evening. In the dark, he loaded his wagon, put her in it, covered her, and drove to the outskirts of another town. There he told her she must get out and directed her to a second station. Mrs. Tatlock says Harriet was handed from one station to another until she reached the North.

It is quite possible that Harriet received such help from sympathetic whites and free blacks, even in the first part of her trip through the slaveholding counties of Maryland. There were settlements of Quakers in Dorchester County and a Friends' Meeting House (or gathering place, like a church) on the Transquaking River, which ran past the Brodess plantation. Friends also met at Federalsburg, Preston, and Concord, towns 20 and 30 miles (32 and 48 km) northeast from Bucktown. Two more meetings, at Denton and Greensboro, were close to the Choptank River.[8]

*This painting of the Underground Railroad
at work shows blacks and whites working
together to ensure freedom for all.*

Thus, Harriet may have been conducted from one Friend to another, but she had other resources to rely on as well. The route to freedom she had heard about from slaves was to follow the Choptank River. If a fugitive followed it west, the Choptank flowed into the Chesapeake, a water highway north to freedom—coming first to Baltimore, then Delaware and Philadelphia. Harriet chose the land route, following the Choptank northeast.

Hiding by day and walking by night, she could follow the Choptank for much of its sixty-seven miles, keeping the North Star in front of her and to the left. The North Star, she often said, was the one thing she was *always* sure of. She had observed, too, that the brooks ran north. Several large tributaries flowed into the Choptank, and Harriet would have walked inland to find a way around them or found a trustworthy person to row her across.

Even with help, Harriet had to depend on her own wits. She had natural cunning and a sense of whom to approach for food or shelter. It seems no one hunted Harriet on this first escape, but she took precautions to hide her tracks. Running water, she knew, "never tells no tales."[9] She never feared the cemeteries and the places the masters had said were haunted. She avoided roads, knowing the swamplands were safer.

As if to counterbalance her sleeping spells, which sometimes overtook her at vulnerable moments, she developed an uncanny sense of approaching danger. Mainly, she trusted in God to lead her on, saying she was "always conscious of an invisible pillar of cloud by day, and of fire by night," under the guidance of which she journeyed or rested.[10]

Where the Choptank becomes merely a stream, she crossed into Delaware, which was still a slaveholding state. Most of the slave owners were in southern Delaware, however, and the Underground Railroad was well developed in northern Delaware. Seventeen rivers led from the Eastern Shore of Maryland into Delaware, with runaways floating down many of them toward freedom. Free blacks outnum-

44

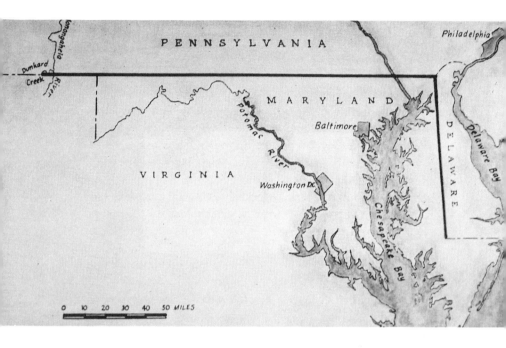

*The Mason-Dixon line divided more than
Maryland and Pennsylvania. For many who
crossed over, it divided slavery from freedom,
for which they had struggled for miles.*

bered slaves in the state by almost ten to one, so there were
friendly hands available if Harriet knew whom to ask.

Just across the border was the Cowgill farm in Willow
Grove, where Henry Cowgill hid runaways in the barn. A
few miles farther, in the town of Camden, was the Camden
meetinghouse, a center of Quaker antislavery activity.
Around the corner a block away, fugitives could rest at the
Cooper House in a bunk-lined secret room above the
kitchen. East of town at Wildcat Manor, Ezekiel Hunn was
notorious to slave catchers for his harboring of fugitives.
Late at night they would be led from a cellar room under the

kitchen down to a landing on the St. Jones's River. From there the slaves were smuggled north under the false floors of the shallops used to ship grain to Delaware Bay.[11]

Ezekiel's brother John in Middletown was just as busy. John Hunn called himself the "chief engineer" of the underground line from Wilmington south. He had been convicted and fined the year before for helping seven runaways. Even after his land holdings and all his possessions were sold at a sheriff's sale to pay his fines, he vowed never to stop his underground activities.

From Camden, black conductors could also have helped Harriet run the gauntlet of towns to the Christiana River and Wilmington, just beyond it. Once in Wilmington, Harriet was but a short distance from the famous Mason-Dixon line, the line between Delaware and Pennsylvania, slavery and freedom—the line she had seen in her dreams.

For the rest of her life Harriet remembered the moment she knew she had crossed the line.

I looked at my hands to see if I was the same person now I was free. There was such a glory over everything. The sun came like gold through the trees and over the fields, and I felt like I was in heaven.[12]

5
A CALLING

Just over the Mason-Dixon line, in southeastern Pennsylvania, lived a nest of abolitionists just waiting to help fugitives reach Philadelphia. The first big city over the line and also a port, Philadelphia had the largest black community in the country in the early 1850s, but there was always room for more. Many boats arriving from Virginia, Maryland, and Delaware carried stowaways who quickly blended into the city's cosmopolitan atmosphere. With help, a fugitive could find advice, work, lodging, and safety.

With or without aid from the abolitionists, Harriet made her way twenty miles from the line to "the crowd and tumult of a great city," whose "glaring brick walls" showed only patches of the sky between. Compared to the slaveholding South, Philadelphia was a haven, but slave catchers occasionally arrived to search for runaways. There was prejudice, too, against the blacks. Charlotte Forten, the well-educated black woman who described the "great city" in her diary, found Philadelphia much more restrictive than New England. She wrote angrily one hot day about an ice-cream parlor that had refused to serve her.[1]

How much more forlorn did Harriet, an illiterate field hand, feel? Where were the lovely ladies in white she had seen in her dreams, holding out their arms? "I had crossed the line of which I had so long been dreaming," she remembered. "I was free—but there was no one to welcome me to the land of freedom. I was a stranger in a strange land, and my home after all was down in the old cabin quarter, with all the folks, and my brothers and sisters."[2]

The first thing Harriet needed was work, and that she was able to find. Private homes and schools and the nearby resort of Cape May, New Jersey, had openings for housekeepers, laundresses, scrubwomen, cooks, and seamstresses. Harriet went through a succession of domestic jobs, glorying in the freedom to quit one job and look for another whenever she wanted to.

With money in her pocket Harriet must have been tempted to buy things for herself, such as dresses and kinds of food she had never been allowed to eat, but she did not glory in spending her hard-earned money. She carefully put it away, making plans for overcoming her loneliness in the North. Members of her family would not dare to come north alone, so she would return to Maryland, she decided, and bring them out, too. She would not be happy, she knew, until "her people" were free.

In her characteristically indirect manner, Harriet later told a story to illustrate why her freedom could not be complete without her family:

> *I knew of a man who was sent to the State Prison for twenty-five years. All these years he was always thinking of his home, and counting by years, months, and days, the time till he should be free, and see his family and friends once more. The years roll on, the time of imprisonment is over, the man is free. He leaves the prison gates, he makes his way to his old home, but his old home is not there. The house in which he had dwelt in his childhood had been torn down, and a new one had been put up in*

48

its place, his family were gone, their very name was
forgotten, there was no one to take him by the hand
to welcome him back to life.

"So it was with me," she said.[3]

For twenty-nine years, Harriet had aimed toward freedom, and she had finally secured it. But she could not enjoy it alone. To return to the South would imperil that freedom, but she did not hesitate. She felt a calling to free other slaves.

I had seen their tears and sighs, and I had heard
their groans, and I would give every drop of blood
in my veins to free them. I was free, and they should
be free also; I would make a home for them in the
North, and the Lord helping me, I would bring them
all there.[4]

She missed Mary Ann, who was either her niece or her half sister. (Mary Ann's mother had been sold farther south, and Mary Ann always called Harriet "Sister Harriet.") Even though Mary Ann worked as a house servant, under the close eye of her mistress, she seemed to have a good chance of escaping. Harriet persuaded someone to write a letter for her to Mary Ann's husband, John Bowley, suggesting a plan.

If Bowley, a free man, could help Mary Ann and their two young children get as far as Baltimore, Harriet would conduct them the rest of the way to Philadelphia. She told John to hire a fishing boat in Cambridge and to be prepared to sail the group up the Chesapeake to Bodkin's Point, where she would meet them. The plan almost fell through, however, on the day chosen for the escape. Mary Ann's master unexpectedly decided to bring her to Cambridge and sell her on the auction block, which was next to the courthouse.

Ninety years later Mary Ann's son, Harkless Bowley, told how his mother was actually sold twice that day. Before noon she was tentatively bid off, Bowley said, but "while the auctioneer went to dinner she was hid in a lady's house only a five-minute walk from the courthouse. When the auctioneers returned, mother was gone." Angered by her escape, he sold her again, sight unseen, to someone who took the chance of coming up empty-handed. Meanwhile, Harkless said,

> *my father, John Bowley, took mother and two children in a small boat to Baltimore. . . . Aunt Harriet had a hiding place there for her, [and] in a few days took her and the children and several others aboard the underground railroad into Canada.*[5]

This was Harriet's first rescue, made in December 1850, a year after her own escape. She did not go far into slave territory this time, but Baltimore was a dangerous city for a fugitive. A law forbade even a free black's leaving by railroad or boat without first being weighed and measured and showing a bond signed by persons who were known locally. Somehow Harriet and her party circumvented this law. Perhaps she had help from two marketwomen in Baltimore who were known to give out passports, or "freedoms," which were used by runaways and then returned to be used again. A trader named Coleman also smuggled slaves out in the six-horse wagon he used to haul merchandise from Baltimore to villages along a turnpike leading into Pennsylvania. Harriet may have bribed a ticket agent or found one who was willing to look the other way.

The next year Harriet went back for her brother John, who was working in Talbot County, just north of Dorchester County. Two other men came along on the escape, but John had to leave his two young sons behind. Later he asked Mary Ann's husband, John Bowley, to return for them, since Bowley was free and could travel without risk of recapture. Bowley kidnapped the boys from their owner, one at a time, and sent them north to their father.

On her third trip, in the fall of 1851, Harriet went all the way back to Dorchester County for John Tubman. Hoping to persuade him to come with her, she had furnished a room for them in Philadelphia. But John Tubman had married again, the year after Harriet had left, and did not want to go.

Harriet was bitterly disappointed. For the rest of her life, she said very little about John Tubman. His rejection seemed to reinforce her determination to link her own happiness to the plight of others. No longer did *her people* mean just family and friends. Spurned by John, she rounded up ten slaves who were desperate for freedom and escorted them north.

In these early rescues, Harriet was shaping a mode of operation that would carry her unscathed through a decade of freeing slaves. She would start out with her groups on a weekend, usually Saturday night, so that the runaways' absence might go unnoticed for a day. No newspapers were published on Sunday, and slave owners would not be able to print handbills announcing the runaways until at least Monday morning. By then Harriet's groups would have two nights of walking behind them. If handbills were posted ahead of them, Harriet would pay someone to follow along and take them down as soon as they were put up.

Harriet used some unusual methods to communicate with her groups. "If I remember correctly," the suffragette Alice Stone Blackwell recalled,

> *Harriet Tubman told me that when she was convoying parties of fugitives, she used to guide them by the songs that she sang as she walked along the roads. . . . It was when her parties of fugitives were in hiding that she directed them by her songs as to whether they might show themselves, or must continue to lie low. . . . No one would notice what was sung by an old colored woman, as she trudged along the road.*[6]

On one such trip with a large party, the pursuit was close and vigorous; the woods were scoured, residents questioned, roads watched, and people were stopped and asked about a band of black fugitives known to be fleeing through that part of the country. Harriet hid her party in the woods, each behind a tree, and left them that night to try to find food. She promised to sing on her return to let them know whether it was safe to come out. If it was unsafe, she would sing:

> Moses, go down in Egypt,
> Tell old Pharaoh, let me go.
> Hadn't been for Adam's fall
> Shouldn't have to have died at all.

If it was safe, she would sing a more hopeful song. After a long time, the party in the woods heard Harriet singing in the distance:

> Hail, oh hail ye happy spirits,
> > Death no more shall make you fear,
> Grief nor sorrow, pain nor anguish
> > Shall no more distress you here.
>
> Around you are ten thousand angels,
> > Always ready to obey command.
> They are always hovering around you,
> > Till you reach the heavenly land.

Undiscovered and heartened by the food she had gathered, the group continued to the "heavenly land."[7]

Harriet used songs not only to communicate but also to calm the fears of the runaways and to give them courage. She herself had no fear of bloodhounds—she had a way with animals—but she did carry paregoric, a form of opium, to keep babies asleep at times when silence was important. She carried the babies herself in a ticking bag around her waist.

Harriet traveled with a gun and sharpened clam shells or stones that could be aimed at a forehead. When a fugitive became hungry, tired, cold, footsore, and scared, and began thinking favorably of his slave home, Harriet would rub his feet and try to calm him first. Then she would bring out the gun and give him a choice, "Live north or die here."

Would she really shoot someone who gave up? she was asked later.

"Yes," she replied with assurance. "If he was weak enough to give out, he'd be weak enough to betray us all, and all who had helped us; and do you think I'd let so many die just for one coward man?"[8]

In the first three trips, Harriet brought her people only as far as Philadelphia, but by 1851 the city was no longer safe. The long-simmering national debate over slavery had resulted in one final attempt to reconcile the North and the South. Under the leadership of Henry Clay and Daniel Webster, Congress had agreed to the Compromise of 1850, which gave the North a few things it wanted—the admission of California as a free state and an end to the slave trade in the District of Columbia—in return for a law that the South wanted, the Fugitive Slave Law.

Abolitionists such as Harriet referred to the years that followed as "the years of terror of the Fugitive Slave Law." Under the new law, any black person could be arrested as a suspected runaway on the accusation of any white person. The issue would go before a special U.S. commissioner, who would decide whether the black person was indeed the "missing property" of the owner who claimed him or her. No lawyers or juries would partake in the hearing. The commissioner was paid five dollars for every black person he turned loose and ten dollars for every one he sent south. Thus slave owners were guaranteed the right to recover their property in the unsympathetic states of the North.

Northern whites were disturbed by the law and shocked when recovered runaways were marched through their streets. People who had avoided thinking about the issue of slavery could no longer do so. Vigilance committees were formed in a number of cities to aid and protect fugitives.

The law produced a panic among blacks, who feared that even a free black could be claimed as a slave solely on the word of a slaveholder. Some began carrying arms, and

CAUTION!!
COLORED PEOPLE
OF BOSTON, ONE & ALL,
You are hereby respectfully **CAUTIONED** and advised, to avoid conversing with the
Watchmen and Police Officers of Boston,
For since the recent ORDER OF THE MAYOR & ALDERMEN, they are empowered to act as
KIDNAPPERS
AND
Slave Catchers,
And they have already been actually employed in **KIDNAPPING, CATCHING, AND KEEPING SLAVES.** Therefore, if you value your **LIBERTY**, and the *Welfare of the Fugitives* among you, *Shun* them in every possible manner, as so many *HOUNDS* on the track of the most unfortunate of your race.

Keep a Sharp Look Out for KIDNAPPERS, and have TOP EYE open.
APRIL 24, 1851.

Posters such as this one warned blacks in northern cities of the new dangers posed by the Fugitive Slave Law.

large groups left the Northern cities for Canada, the only place where former slaves were safe from recapture. The British government had proclaimed in 1833 that all colored people living on Canadian soil were free. "After that I wouldn't trust Uncle Sam with my people no longer," Harriet said, "but I brought them all clear off to Canada."[9]

In her first rescues, Harriet seems to have acted alone, with some help from a literate friend in Philadelphia. She relied on the experience of her own escape, and she must have known of safe shelters in Maryland and Delaware when she brought out the groups in 1851. On her fourth trip, and the last one in 1851, Harriet returned to Dorchester County in December and called out her brother James, his wife, and nine others. By then she had met ex-slave and editor Frederick Douglass, who had escaped from Maryland thirteen years before and started an abolitionist newspaper. She stopped at his house in Rochester, New York, with the party of eleven on the way to St. Catharines in Canada.[10]

After the Fugitive Slave Law, when the length of the trip to freedom more than doubled and the chances of recapture extended all the way to the Canadian border, Harriet needed more than her own resources to take her parties to the welcoming arms of Queen Victoria. In order to continue her work, it was time to link up with the chief engineers on the Underground Railroad.

6
"MOSES"

Steep, wooden steps at the back of an old building in Philadelphia led to the "office" of the Philadelphia Vigilance
Committee, one of the committees that had responded to the
Fugitive Slave Law with help for runaways. This office was
the main eastern station on the Underground Railroad.
There, in the loft, a black man named William Still welcomed newly arrived fugitives. His job for the committee
was to determine whether an applicant was indeed a runaway and to offer whatever was needed—food, clothing,
shelter, or news of relatives who had come north earlier.
Still had discovered in one such interview that the fugitive
standing before him was his very own brother, one of two
children left behind when his mother escaped slavery.[1]

After that Still kept extensive records of the interviews,
hoping they might reunite other families. He wrote down
how many were in the party, their names, their physical
descriptions, and the names of their masters and the county
they ran away from. He asked them questions about their
escape experiences and the severity of their lives as slaves.
When helping runaways became especially dangerous, Still
hid the records in a graveyard. After the Civil War these

records provided some of the sparse written evidence of Harriet Tubman's work underground.[2]

Harriet had climbed those steps to meet William Still by at least 1852. She may have asked him to write the letter that described the plan for Mary Ann's escape. She may have learned from him the names of the marketwomen in Baltimore who gave out "freedoms." Whatever she learned from Still, he was impressed with her courage and daring and her willingness to put herself in danger to free others. When she began to make frequent trips south, he and the committee provided support. She would stay with his family on her way there, then bring parties of fugitives up the stairs to be recorded and aided in their trip farther north.

Despite Still's systematic approach, the Underground Railroad was really just a loose network of people willing to help. It was called the Underground Railroad (or Road) because its work was conducted in secret, usually at night, and slaves eluded slave catchers "as if swallowed up by an underground passage."[3]

The network could have begun operation as early as the 1780s, when George Washington complained about escaping slaves. It was especially active in cities and towns close to border states. Maryland citizens complained to the governors of Delaware, Pennsylvania, and New Jersey in 1798 and 1815 that citizens of those states were helping slaves to escape. They were undoubtedly right. Fugitives headed for the homes of known abolitionists or to black communities, particularly in Cincinnati, Philadelphia, and Wilmington. William Brinkley, a free black man in Camden, Delaware, wrote to Still in 1857 that "Harrat . . . stops at my house when she passes. . . ."[4]

Quakers, Wesleyan Methodists, and Reformed Presbyterians were well known for their involvement in the Underground, but many other people quietly provided a night's lodging or a ride to the next town. Most acted out of conscience, the belief that a slave's right to freedom was greater than the property rights guaranteed by the Constitution.

Over the years of its existence, the Underground Railroad helped from forty thousand to one hundred thousand slaves to reach the North (four million more remained slaves).[5] By the 1850s, when Harriet became a conductor, the help network was in full operation. But most fugitives still had to complete the hardest part of the journey—the first part—on their own. Harriet was one of the few agents willing to go to the South, to recruit an escape party, and to escort it the complete distance.

Harriet usually made two trips a year, in the spring and the fall. She worked during the winter and summer to earn money. In addition to the four trips she made in 1850 and 1851, Harriet returned to the Eastern Shore of Maryland at least eight times in the following five years. These are trips mentioned either in Still's records or in the letters of Thomas Garrett, her underground contact in Wilmington, Delaware. Altogether, Harriet said she made nineteen trips south, conducting about a hundred people out before the Civil War.

Harriet's routes were fixed in her head, not on a map, and she varied the course when she needed to, relying on her own ingenuity. In 1897 she was interviewed by Wilbur Siebert, who wrote a book about the Underground Railroad (URR).[6] She told Siebert that she had made use of URR stations in Delaware at Camden, Dover, Blackbird, Middleton, New Castle, and Wilmington, as well as Laurel, Milford, Millsborough, Concord, Seaford, Smyrna, and Delaware City.

Harriet needed that many stations because there were many dangerous towns to avoid, towns where proslavery sentiments prevailed. William Brinkley in Camden called Dover and Smyrna "the two worst places on this side of the Maryland line."[7]

Those who helped did so at some risk, but there were always people willing to help. On one trip, Harriet and a band of runaways arrived early in the morning at the home of a free black man who usually sheltered her parties. Leaving her group huddled together in the pouring rain, Harriet went to the door with her customary knock. Hearing no

*Harriet, far left, poses with a group of
ex-slaves whose escape she had orchestrated.*

response, she knocked again, several times. A white man raised a window and gruffly asked what she wanted. When she mentioned her friend, she was told that he had been forced to leave for "harboring niggers."

Knowing that she had raised an alarm, Harriet cast about quickly for a place to hide her group. She remembered a spot outside of town, an island in a swamp with tall grass. Carrying twin babies in the bag under her arm, she led the group wading in the swamp and ordered them to lie down in the tall, wet grass. There they hid—cold, damp, and hungry all day—while Harriet prayed for help.

After dusk a man dressed in Quaker garb came walking slowly along the pathway at the edge of the swamp. He seemed to be talking to himself: "My wagon stands in the barnyard of the next farm across the way. The horse is in the stable; the harness hangs on a nail." When night fell, Harriet found the wagon, stocked with food, and her party rode safely to the next station.[8] Such deliverances strengthened Harriet's faith that God was on her side. The deliverance was also testimony to the effective communication system of the Underground.

Harriet believed that money, too, would be provided by God through earthly channels. One person she could always count on for help was the Quaker Thomas Garrett, an iron and hardware merchant in Wilmington. Garrett's sympathy for fugitives began when he returned home one day at the age of twenty-five to find his family dismayed and indignant at the kidnapping of a black woman in their employ. After that he never failed to help a fugitive; he claimed to have aided more than 2,700 men, women, and children who passed through Wilmington on their way across the line.

Garrett's store at 227 Shipley Street was a clearinghouse of information for the Underground Railroad. In the back room he wrote letters to the nest of abolitionists in Chester County, Pennsylvania, about passengers he was passing along to them. He kept in touch with agents south of him in Delaware about who was on the way. Because he made no secret of his activities, his house and store were constantly watched by the police, but the free black community of Wilmington watched, too, and alerted him to danger.

We know from his letters that Harriet had stopped at Garrett's by December 1854, but they may have met earlier. From 1854 on, she checked in with him often and relied on his resources. As soon as she and her parties were within a few miles of Wilmington, Garrett would have agents scouting the road so he could help them cross the bridge over the Christiana River, which was watched by slave catchers. From Wilmington, many hands in Chester County would help fugitives along to Philadelphia, for as Garrett remarked, "they're all abolitionists there."[9] Garrett described Harriet's exploits and courage to abolitionists in the North and abroad, and members of the Anti-Slavery Society of Edinburgh, Scotland, sent money.

One letter from Scotland in 1857 included five British pounds designated for Harriet Tubman. Garrett had not heard from Harriet for several weeks, so he left a note with William Still, informing her of the donation. She walked into Garrett's store that fall and was directed to the back where he was writing.

I said to her, "Harriet, I am glad to see thee. Thee looks much better than when I last saw thee."

Her reply was, "Yes, I thank you. I am now well, and God has sent me to you for money."

Deciding to tease her a bit, Garrett replied,

"Harriet, how is this? I expected thee would want a new pair of shoes, as usual, when thee has been on a journey. These I can give thee, but thee know I have a great many calls for money from the coloured people, and thee cannot expect much money from me."

Her reply was, "You can give me what I need, now. God never fools me."

61

So he asked her how much she wanted. She said she needed three and a half shillings for shoes for herself, for a woman she had just brought out, and for their passage to Philadelphia; she needed twenty shillings to go back to the Eastern Shore for her sister and children.

> *"Harriet, has thee been to Philadelphia, lately?"* Garrett asked, wondering if she had received his message.
>
> *"No,"* she answered.
>
> *"Has anyone told thee I had money for thee?"*
>
> *"No, nobody but God."*

Garrett then gave her 24 shillings and 31 cents, the proceeds of the five pounds sent for her. The timing and the amount of the gift confirmed Harriet's belief that God would provide.[10]

As Harriet's work became better known, ex-slaves began asking her to bring out members of their families. Slaves desperate to escape waited for the word that she was in their neighborhood, rounding up another party. Harriet herself became increasingly concerned about the rest of her family. Her parents seemed in no immediate danger, but late in 1854, she "became much troubled in spirit about her brothers" still in Maryland—Benjamin, Henry, and Robert. She had received a warning, either from Still or in a dream, that they were about to be sold. She asked a friend to write a letter to Jacob Jackson, a literate black man who lived near the plantation where her brothers were working.

Because Jackson's mail was watched, Harriet dictated the letter as if it were from an adopted son, William Henry Jackson, who lived in the North. After some ordinary news, "William Henry" wrote:

> *Read my letter to the old folks, and give my love to them, and tell my brothers to be always watching*

62

unto prayer, and when the good old ship of Zion
comes along, to be ready to step on board.

But Jackson's folks were dead, and he had no sons, so the authorities were suspicious. They sent for Jackson, who read the letter slowly, threw it down, and said, "That letter can't be meant for me no how; I can't make head or tail of it." Then he let Harriet's brothers know that she was on the way.[11]

The sale of her brothers was set for Monday, the day after Christmas, 1854. Harriet arrived in Dorchester County and established contact with the brothers, who were still owned by Brodess's widow, Eliza Ann. She told them to start immediately after dark on Christmas Eve for their father's and mother's cabin. Rit and Ben then lived 40 miles (64 km) away on one of Doc Thompson's farms in Caroline County. Harriet knew of three others who wanted to flee and would join them: John Chase, Peter Jackson, and Jane Kane.

Harriet's brother Henry, however, had a wife and a child. His wife was about to have their second child, and on Christmas Eve she went into labor. Harriet wouldn't wait. She and the five others left as planned.

Henry waited until the baby was born and then tried to leave, but his wife was wary. He had not told her about the possibility of sale or of his plans to escape. Finally, he told her he was going to try to get hired out to another man, as Christmas was the day such changes were made. "Oh, Henry," she said, "you're going to leave me. I know it. But wherever you go, don't forget me and the children." Promising to send Harriet back for them later, Henry hurried to catch up with the others.[12]

The party spent Christmas Day among ears of corn in a fodder house next to the Ross cabin. They dared not show themselves to Rit, who might raise a ruckus. Harriet sent John Chase to fetch her father and some food. Even Ben would not look his daughter in the face; he knew he would be questioned later, and he wanted to be able to say that he had not "seen" his children.

All day it rained, and all day Rit waited for the sons she expected to visit for Christmas. Through the chinks in the boards of the fodder house, they saw her come to the door every few minutes and take a long look down the road. At nightfall, just before it was time to leave, Harriet crept to the window of the cabin for a look at her mother, who was sitting by the fire with a pipe in her mouth and her head on her hand, rocking back and forth in her chair.

Ben said his good-byes with a bandanna tied over his eyes, and the party set out. When their escape was discovered the next day, Ben said he "hadn't seen one of 'em this Christmas." Rit said she'd been looking for them all day and "not one of 'em came this Christmas."[13]

Traveling mainly on foot for more than 100 miles, (161 km) the group arrived at Garrett's in Wilmington. Harriet and one of the men "had worn their shoes off their feet," so Garrett gave them two dollars to buy new ones and hired a carriage to take them on to Philadelphia. They reached St. Catharines, Canada, early in 1855.

From rescues such as this grew the legend of a conductor known as Moses. When the brothers stopped in Philadelphia, William Still wrote in his book that

Harriet Tubman had been their Moses. . . . She had faithfully gone down into Egypt and delivered these six bondsmen by her own heroism. Her like, it is probable, was never known before. . . .[14]

William Wells Brown, black writer and journalist, interviewed some of the exiles in Canada.

Men from Canada, who had made their escape years before, and whose families were still in the prison-house of slavery, would seek out Moses, and get her to go and bring their dear ones away. How strange! This woman—one of the most ordinary

64

looking of her race; unlettered; no idea of geography, asleep half of the time. . . . No fugitive was ever captured who had Moses for a leader.

That was the key to the legend. There were dozens of conductors on the Underground Railroad, some of whom rescued more people than Harriet. But most of them did not get by untouched; many were jailed, and a few were killed.

"Were you not afraid of being caught?" Brown asked one successful fugitive.

"O, no," said he, "Moses is got de charm."

"What do you mean?"

"De whites can't catch Moses, kase you see she's born wid de charm. De Lord has given Moses de power."

Harriet herself felt she had the charm. It "nerved her up, gave her courage, and made all who followed her feel safe in her hands."[15] God would protect her, she thought, because she never went without his consent or approbation.

"The Lord told me to do this. I said, 'O Lord, I can't—don't ask me—take somebody else.' Then I could hear the Lord answer, 'It's you I want, Harriet Tubman'—just as clear as I heard him speak—and then I'd go again down South and bring up my brothers and sisters."[16]

7

PURSUIT

In November 1856, Harriet's father, Ben Ross, received word that the next time "Moses" came round, Josiah Bailey was ready to flee. Five feet, ten inches tall, well-built, with an "intelligent countenance," Joe was a valuable slave. His sudden desire to escape flamed when he received a severe flogging.

The flogging was given not for any offense Joe had committed but to teach him to respect a new master. For six years Joe had been hired out to a planter who had used him as an overseer. The planter valued Joe's work so much he became determined to buy him—for $1,000 down and $1,000 later. Regardless of Joe's value, however, the new master's first lesson to his slaves was that "I am master and they belong to me and are never to resist anything I order them to do. So I always begin by giving them a good licking." Joe took the licking but resolved it would be his last, even if it meant leaving his wife and three children behind.

Freedom was a painful choice for a slave. Those who left often vowed to return and rescue their family later, as Harriet's brother John had done. All knew that their masters—at any time—could sell them and send them away from their families. Running at least gave them some control of their own lives and a chance for a reunion later in the North.

Self-respect was important to Joe. By the time Harriet came, he had persuaded his older brother Bill to leave, too. Harriet had really come for her sister, but the sister could not get two of her children away from another plantation, and she refused to leave without them. Harriet promised to return during the Christmas holidays, when the children might be allowed to visit their mother. She took Joe, Bill, Peter Pennington, Eliza Nokey, and one other slave with her instead.

As was Harriet's custom, the party left on a Saturday night, November 15, to get in a day of travel before their flight would be discovered. The pursuit was quick. Rewards of $1,500 were advertised in an Eastern Shore newspaper for anyone who could apprehend Joe and land him safely in the Easton jail; $800 was offered for Peter and $300 for Bill. An additional reward of $12,000 was offered for the capture of this man "Moses" who was said to be stealing valuable property.[1]

Hiding by day in holes dug under house floors to store potatoes, the escaping party traveled 90 miles on foot in six nights, at one point separating and meeting up again at the home of a black Methodist minister, the Reverend Samuel Green. Passing through a string of towns in Delaware, they reached South Wilmington and found shelter there with free blacks.

Three days before they arrived, the masters of Joe, Peter, and Bill had posted handbills in the area. But they "were torn down by the colored people as fast as they were put up," Thomas Garrett wrote to a friend in Scotland. "They also had them distributed at the railway depots, and principle [sic] towns all the way to where they left."[2]

With all bridges being watched and even some residents on the lookout for the fugitives, hoping to earn the rewards, Harriet sent a message to Garrett asking for help crossing the Christiana River into Wilmington. Garrett devised a clever ploy. He sent two wagons out of the city in the morning carrying a load of straw and a group of bricklayers who behaved as though they were headed for an outing. When the bricklayers returned that night, they acted as if they had been drinking all day. The police let them pass without bothering to inspect the wagon, where Harriet and her five fugitives lay hidden under the straw.[3]

Delivered safely to Garrett's store, they were supplied with all needed equipment, including shoes, and sent on their way to the Chester County abolitionists. At his office in Philadelphia, Still wrote detailed descriptions of the men, especially Joe, and wrote that the party's spirits never flagged. They were on their way to Canada.

Their spirits changed in New York. Handbill descriptions of the runaways had been sent ahead to the New York Anti-Slavery Office, and when Joe walked in, Oliver Johnson startled him by saying, "Well I'm glad to see the man whose head is worth fifteen hundred dollars." Realizing how easily he might still be recognized, Joe was plunged into gloom.

Four days after they left Wilmington, Garrett received a letter from Johnson saying the party had departed that morning by train to Canada. Soon they would be in "that cold and dreary land" where "a man's a man by law." But "from that time, Joe was silent; he talked no more; he sang no more; he sat with his head on his hand, and nobody could rouse him, nor make him take any interest in anything."

The usual "underground" route from New York City was to take the train to Albany, then Syracuse, and Rochester, then across the Niagara River to Canada. As they crossed the Suspension Bridge over the river, the rest of the groups sang "the Canada song" about the iron horse bearing them over to freedom, but Joe would not even look at the famous Niagara Falls. Harriet knew from a slight descent on the Canadian side of the bridge when they had crossed the border. She sprang to Joe's side and shook him: "Joe, you've shook the lion's paw. Joe, you're free!"

Finally aroused, Joe looked up, raised his hands, and broke out in song, with tears streaming down his face:

Glory to God and Jesus too;
One more soul is safe!
Oh, go and carry the news;
One more soul got safe!

Still singing loudly, Joe stepped out of the railroad car and said there was only one more trip for him, to heaven. Harriet Tubman barked, "Well, you old fool, you! You might at least have looked at the falls first and gone to heaven afterwards!"[4]

The successful escape of Joe and the other slaves came at a cost of more than three thousand dollars in property for their owners. The area around Bucktown, in particular, had lost many slaves. In newspaper offices in the North, it was common knowledge that "the Bucktown-Cambridge region was being plucked of slaves like a chicken of its feathers before roasting."[5]

When individual masters failed to recover their escaped slaves, the slaveholders of the Eastern Shore decided to act collectively. Right after a large group of slaves fled Cambridge in October 1857, Dorchester County slave owners organized a society of slaveholders, which held a convention in Cambridge the next year. One of their goals was the reenslavement of free blacks, who were seen as encouraging slaves to run.

In June of 1859 a statewide convention met. The convention found it "inexpedient" to expel all the free blacks from the area because their labor was needed, but it did come up with one unique idea—insurance policies for slaves. The Southern Slaveholders' Insurance Company of Maryland guaranteed that insured slaves who ran away would either be returned or their value paid to the owner. The Maryland legislature considered offering a reward for the capture of Thomas Garrett, but Garrett was unperturbed. "I have not yet been kidnapped by the Marylanders," he wrote after the session.[6]

Maryland slaveholders also tracked Harriet with a vengeance. The price on her head rose. Some writers have said that rewards as high as forty thousand dollars (more than half a million dollars in modern currency) were offered for Harriet Tubman. No newspaper advertisements or handbills have been found to substantiate this claim, however, other than the twelve-thousand-dollar ad mentioned by Still. The forty-thousand-dollar sum is probably a total of all the rewards offered at various times, but even twelve thousand dollars is high for a "sickly" slave once said to be worth only two hundred dollars.[7]

Harriet did have some narrow escapes. Once she was traveling north alone by train, having sent her party of fugitives on the Underground Railroad. She heard her name spoken and froze under her sunbonnet as a passenger standing beside her read aloud a poster offering a reward for a runaway slave named Harriet Tubman. She kept her head down, got off at the next station, and took a train going south, figuring no one would suspect a fugitive of traveling south.

Harriet was adept at disguise. Sometimes she dressed as a man. Then the mistaken impression that "Moses" was a man helped her to escape when she dressed again as a woman. Once back in the Bucktown vicinity, where her face was known, she "pulled her sunbonnet over her face and imitated the gait of an elderly person. In the marketplace she bought a pair of live fowls. Turning a corner, she met a man to whom she had once been 'hired out.' She twitched the string that bound the legs of the chickens, and as they struggled and screamed, she bent over them and so hid her face as she went by her master."[8]

Harriet also maintained that she had premonitions of danger, a claim backed by Thomas Garrett, who told of a close call near Smyrna, Delaware:

In one instance, when she had several stout men with her, some thirty miles below here, she said that God told her to stop, which she did; and then asked him what she must do. He told her to leave the road and turn to the left; she obeyed, and soon came to a small stream of tide water; there was no boat, no bridge; she again inquired of her Guide what she was to do. She was told to go through. It was cold, in the month of March, but having confidence in her Guide, she went in; the water came up to her armpits; the men refused to follow till they saw her safe on the opposite shore. They then followed, and if I mistake not, she had soon to wade a second stream, and soon after which she came to a cabin of colored people, who took them all in, put them to bed, and dried their clothes, ready to proceed next night on their journey. Harriet had run out of money, and gave them some of her underclothing to pay for their kindness.

"When she called on me two days after," Garrett wrote, "she was so hoarse she could hardly speak, and was also suffering with violent toothache." Afterward, she found out that advertisements had been put up on the road ahead and patrollers were watching for them.[9]

In March 1857 a group of eight slaves fled from Harriet's old neighborhood, led by a Thomas Otwell who had once made a trip north with Harriet. Otwell used his association with Harriet and his knowledge of the underground routes to gain the slaves' confidence, but in the middle of the night he led them unaware straight to the jail in Dover, Delaware, hoping to collect a reward.

When the slaves were taken to a room where the windows were barred with iron, they became suspicious and stepped out into the hall. The sheriff came upstairs, expecting to turn the key in the lock, but encountered the fugitives in the hall instead and ran downstairs for his pistols. The

*Although looking like herself here,
Harriet was great at disguises, which made
her work as "Moses" a little easier.*

eight followed; one picked up a hot andiron from the hearth and kept the sheriff at bay while the rest broke out the window and jumped 12 feet (3.6 m) to soft mud.[10] They scattered in different directions, and after an anxious two weeks of watching, Still reported that they had all arrived safely in Philadelphia.

Although Otwell was found out and the slaves escaped, several underground operators were betrayed to the authorities in the process. One was William Brinkley, at whose house Otwell had stopped with Harriet. Brinkley seems to have survived the betrayal, perhaps because Delaware was more tolerant of runaways and those who helped them than Maryland was. Another free black man, the Reverend Samuel Green, did not escape punishment. Green's son, Samuel Green, Jr., had been a slave in Indian Creek, Maryland, but escaped in 1854, inspired, he told Still, by Harriet Tubman.[11] Reverend Green decided to pay a visit to his son in Canada in 1856. The authorities were irked by Sam Jr.'s escape, and when his father returned, they began watching his house.

That November Green harbored Harriet's party of five, including Josiah Bailey. She may have used his house in Dorchester County at other times as a staging point. Shortly after the Dover jailbreak in March, ''a party of gentlemen'' raided Green's cabin. They found a map of Canada, several schedules of routes to the North, a copy of *Uncle Tom's Cabin,* and a letter from Green's son. The letter concluded with a request to tell certain other slaves, and Sam Jr. named them, to come on to Canada. Shortly afterward, those slaves had left.

Reverend Green was found not guilty (on a legal technicality) of having the map, schedule, and letter in his possession, so he was arraigned on possession of the book. This popular novel written by Harriet Beecher Stowe had deeply angered the South with its unfavorable portrayal of slavery. Green, found guilty of having a copy of the book in his possession, was sentenced to ten years in prison.[12]

During the same period Thomas Garrett became concerned about Harriet, too. He sent a worried letter to William Still:

> *I have been very anxious for some time past, to hear what has become of Harriet Tubman. The last I heard of her, she was in the State of New York, on her way to Canada with some friends, last fall. Has thee seen or heard anything of her lately? It would be a sorrowful fact, if such a hero as she, should be lost from the Underground Rail Road.*

Two days later, Still wrote back that Harriet had just arrived in Philadelphia, on her way south again. "I was truly glad to learn that Harriet Tubman was still in good health and ready for action," Garrett wrote back, "but I think there will be more danger at present than heretofore, there is so much excitement below in consequence of the escape of those eight slaves."[13]

The "excitement below," in fact, was the reason for Harriet's trip. She was worried about her parents. Ben Ross was free, and he had purchased Rit's freedom two years before for twenty dollars—she was too old to be of much value. Yet ever since Harriet brought her three brothers out in 1854, Ben had been under suspicion. Harriet received word that he was in trouble, that he was about to be arrested, in fact, for sheltering the eight slaves involved in the Dover jailbreak. (They had stayed in his hut the first day of their escape.) It would tax even Harriet's powers to free Ben from jail, so she hurried south in June to "remove my father's trial to a higher court."

This rescue would not be easy. Once strong and independent, Ben was in his sixties now, with less spring in his walk. He would not leave without Rit, and they could not make it on foot.

Desperate for money, Harriet went to the New York Anti-Slavery Office after telling one of her friends, "I'm not going to eat or drink till I get enough money to take me down after the old people." Once in the office, she demanded twenty dollars but was told they didn't have that much on hand. She sat down and went to sleep, all morning and afternoon. A few times she was urged to leave, but she replied, "No, sir. I'm not going till I get my twenty dollars." By afternoon, sixty dollars had been raised.[14]

She arrived in Maryland just in time; her father was scheduled to appear in court the following day, on Monday. Gathering materials on hand, Harriet constructed a "freedom chariot" from the skeleton of an old buggy, two wheels, and an axle. Across the axle she put a board to sit on. Another board, swung with ropes fastened to the axle, provided a place to rest their feet. She appropriated an old horse and fitted it with a harness collar she made from straw.

Thus outfitted, the three of them rode all night. The next day, in southern Delaware, she put her parents on a train to Wilmington. She continued on alone, driving the chariot. "She turned Jehu herself," Garrett writes, "and drove to town in a style that no human being ever did before or since; but she was happy at having arrived safe."[15] Garrett gave the three money for train fare to Canada, then sold the horse and sent them the proceeds. Ben and Rit were soon reunited with their sons and daughters in Canada.

Except for one sister, Harriet had freed all of Ben and Rit's children by the end of 1857. As North and South moved ever farther apart on the slavery question, the danger of capture increased. Over a decade of increasing risk, Harriet never lost a passenger on the trains she conducted. Nevertheless, she was urged to abandon her underground work to speak against slavery in the North. She would make at least one more trip south before war broke out but would never succeed in rescuing her sister and her sister's children.

8
GENERAL TUBMAN

That first winter in Canada was hard on Ben and Rit. The seven hundred ex-slaves in the community of St. Catharines were friendly, but the weather was bone-chilling cold. They were both too old to work, so Harriet found odd jobs to support them.

The most common work she and other exiles found in Canada was hard physical labor—chopping wood in the snowy forests, clearing land, and doing chores for farmers. The Canadian government encouraged immigrants to buy fifty-acre lots for twenty-one dollars an acre, with ten years to pay. Most of the thirty to forty thousand Negroes who came, however, settled in the towns between Lake Ontario and Lake Erie because they couldn't afford to move farther. Also, they wanted to remain close to the U.S. border. Each year about five hundred would secretly return to the United States to bring away wives and children. Some asked Harriet to do it for them.

Harriet had spent part of each year in St. Catharines, safe "under the paw of the British Lion," since she brought her brother James, his wife, and nine others to Canada in 1851. Most of her family was living in or near the town. In

October 1857, Harriet returned to Maryland to rescue yet another brother, William, and his fiancée Catherine. They also settled nearby.[1]

The names and number of Harriet's brothers and sisters have never been certain, but about this time a lot of people began to call her Aunt Harriet. She assumed responsibility for her parents, sometimes for her brothers, and often for nieces and nephews. In her later years, Harriet raised several children herself. The most curious "Aunt Harriet" story comes, however, from a woman named Alice Brickler, who said that Harriet "kidnapped" her mother, Margaret Stewart, when Margaret was a small girl. Margaret would have been Harriet's niece, the daughter of one of her brothers and a free black woman.

"My mother's life really began with Aunt Harriet kidnapping her from her home on Eastern Shore, Maryland, when she was a little girl eight or nine years old," wrote Alice Brickler. Harriet came to visit and

fell in love with the little girl who was my mother. Maybe it was because in mother she saw the child she herself might have been if slavery had been less cruel. Maybe it was because she knew the joys of motherhood would never be hers and she longed for some little creature who would love her for her own self's sake. Certainly whatever her emotion, it was stronger than her better judgment, for when her visit was ended, she, secretly, and without so much as a by-your-leave, took the little girl with her to her Northern home. . . .

"They made the trip by water," Brickler continued,

as that was what impressed mother so greatly that she forgot to weep over her separation from her twin brother, her mother. . . . Harriet must have regretted her act. . . . She knew she had violated her brother's home and sorrow and anger was there.

77

Harriet must have been desperate for someone to call her own, but she could not change her mission. She was traveling back and forth too often in the mid-1850s to settle down and raise a child. She placed Margaret in the care of Mrs. William H. Seward, wife of the ex-governor of New York, with whom she was friends.[2] The Sewards were residents of Auburn, New York, where Harriet could stop on her travels.

Through her work, Harriet had come to know many of the great abolitionists of the day, and they often enlisted her aid in the antislavery effort in the North. First, she met the New York abolitionists, whose homes were semisecret stops on the Underground Railroad. There was Seward, who had been governor of New York from 1838 to 1842, but is better known in history as being the secretary of state who negotiated the purchase of Alaska—''Seward's Folly,'' as it came to be known—from the Russians. Seward was elected to the U.S. Senate in 1848, where he argued against the Compromise of 1850 and its Fugitive Slave Law, attacking slavery on moral, not just constitutional, grounds. The senator had his eye on the Republican nomination for president in 1860.

Seward was a close friend of Frederick Douglass, who had started an abolitionist weekly in Rochester called the *North Star*. Douglass was the one who kept in touch with Harriet when she traveled through New York. The October 29, 1858, issue of his newspaper carried the cryptic message that ''A valuable parcel left in our care by Rev. Dr. Willis of Toronto awaits the call of Harriet Tubman.'' The parcel was probably a gift of money from the Anti-Slavery Society of Canada. When in Rochester, Harriet would often stay with the Douglasses, at the African Methodist Episcopal Zion Church, or at the home of women's rights advocate Susan B. Anthony.

In Syracuse, the Reverend Jermain Loguen, an ex-slave who escaped from Tennessee in about 1835, sheltered Harriet's groups in his home and church. Because of his helping some fifteen hundred slaves on to Canada, Loguen was known as the ''Underground Railroad King.''

78

Another underground stop was the barn and kitchen of the Peterboro estate of Gerrit Smith. Smith was a millionaire. His father had been the partner of the fur baron, John Jacob Astor, and Smith supported radical causes and the rise of the antislavery Republican party. Elizabeth Cady Stanton visited Smith's estate each year, as did the Oneida Indians from whom Smith's father had purchased large tracts of land. At his home, Harriet met what Mrs. Stanton called "choice society from every part of the country."

Although poor and unlettered, Harriet was admired and accepted by the educated and sometimes wealthy antislavery advocates she visited. "I remember once after I had brought some colored people from the South, I went up to Peterboro to the Big House," Harriet said. "Gerrit Smith's son, Grune, was going hunting with his tutor and some other boys. I had no shoes. It was on Saturday afternoon and—would you believe it?—those boys went right off to the village and got me a pair of shoes so I could go with them."[3]

Harriet's friendship with abolitionists led, in the spring of 1858, to her meeting a white man whose propensity for direct action matched her own. His name was John Brown. Early in his life, Brown had dedicated himself to freeing the slaves. His raid at Harpers Ferry, in what is now West Virginia, would act as a trigger to the Civil War.

Brown had earned a reputation for violent action in Kansas, which had once been Indian Territory. When Kansas was opened for white settlement, Congress gave the settlers the right to vote whether their state would be free or slaveowning. Five thousand Southerners crossed the border to sway the vote, so Brown and his sons came, too, with financial backing and rifles from the Massachusetts State Kansas Committee. Bloody conflicts followed.[4]

Impatient at the impasse in Kansas, Brown was speaking quietly but earnestly that spring to his supporters in New England. The time for political action was over, he argued. If enough slaves could be spirited away from the South, he reasoned, the slave system would collapse. To accomplish this, he wanted to establish a series of fortified Underground Railroad stations in the Appalachian Mountains of Virginia or Tennessee. From these stations, a fighting force of young white men and escaped slaves would raid the plantations and help thousands of slaves to flee.

Brown asked Franklin B. Sanborn, a Boston teacher and intellectual, Unitarian ministers Thomas Higginson and Theodore Parker, and Gerrit Smith for their money and support. They were four of the "Secret Six," a committee formed to aid Brown.[5] He also wanted the help of free blacks such as Douglass and Loguen in recruiting young men. Douglass was only mildly enthusiastic about Brown's plan, but he knew the ideal person to talk to about helping slaves escape. He urged Brown to go to Canada and seek out Harriet Tubman.

Brown had long been curious about Tubman, and he was tremendously impressed with her when Loguen introduced them in April. "The first I see is General Tubman, the second is General Tubman, and the third is General Tubman," he said, shaking her hand three times.[6] Besides the honorific title, Brown paid her what he thought was the supreme compliment of referring to her as a man. "He is the most of a man," Brown wrote to his son, "naturally, that I ever met with."[7]

Harriet had a dream before she met Brown. She was in

a wilderness sort of place, all full of rocks and bushes, when she saw a serpent raise its head among the rocks, and as it did so, it became the head of an old man with a long white beard, gazing at her, "wishful like, just as if he were going to speak to me," and then two other heads rose up beside him, younger than he, and as she stood looking at them, and wondering what they could want with her, a great crowd of men rushed in and struck down the younger heads, and then the head of the old man, still looking at her so "wishful."[8]

When she met Brown, he was the very image of the head she had seen. Sixty years old but agile and alert, he was "lean, strong and sinewy," Douglass wrote, "straight as a mountain pine, built for times of trouble. His eyes were gray and were full of light and fire."[9] With his flowing white beard, he looked like a cross between a Quaker and a warrior.

Harriet, too, was impressed. Here was a white man who was willing to endanger himself to free her people. She told him what she knew about the underground routes and the Virginia terrain, and she agreed to enlist recruits among freed men in Canada. She would be there, she promised, to help guide slaves north when the raids began.

Brown had hoped to put his plan into action that spring, but his New England supporters became hesitant. One of Brown's associates, a military adventurer who had fought in Europe, threatened to betray the plan. The Secret Six urged Brown to delay and henceforth to keep them in the dark about his exact plans. They even stated, in writing, that the rifles purchased by the Massachusetts State Kansas Committee were not to be used outside of Kansas.

After Brown returned to Kansas, Harriet decided that she must find a better home for her parents than the cold climate of Canada. Governor Seward knew of a parcel of land with a small house that was to be auctioned off in his hometown of Auburn, New York. Auburn was a small, friendly town and a center of abolitionist and women's suffrage activity. The property was south of town on the South Street road beyond the tollgate. Harriet told Seward how much money she had, and Seward told the auctioneer there would be "a little black woman sitting in the back and when she made a bid, he was to cut off the bidding."[10] The bidding was stopped at five hundred dollars, which was probably a down payment. Harriet's parents moved in that fall.

Supporting her parents and paying off the mortgage on the house began to consume much of Harriet's energy. Partly out of financial need and at the urging of New York abolitionists, she visited Boston in the winter of 1858–1859 to solicit funds. Gerrit Smith gave her letters of introduction, which she had delivered to important abolitionists. Wanting to be sure she could trust those who came to call on her, Harriet brought along daguerrotypes (small portraits that were the forerunner of the photograph) of her New York friends. If the visitor recognized the likeness, then it was all right to proceed.

Harriet made an impact on all the people she met, and they raised money to pay off her debts. John Brown, who was in Boston again, trying to revive backing for his plan, introduced her to the famous orator Wendell Phillips. "Mr. Phillips, I bring you one of the best and bravest persons on this continent, General Tubman, as we call her," Brown said as he entered Phillips's home with Harriet.[11] She could lead an army as well as any military man that ever lived, Brown insisted. Phillips became her staunch friend and supporter.

When she met Thomas Higginson, he wrote to his mother that

We have had the greatest heroine of the age here, a black woman and a fugitive slave. . . . Her tales of adventure are beyond anything in fiction and her generalship is extraordinary. She had a reward of $12,000 offered for her in Maryland and will probably be burned alive whenever she is caught.

Indeed, Harriet was in great danger in 1859, the year Maryland slaveholders met in convention. Higginson wrote:

An added reward had been put upon her head, with various threats of the different cruel devices by which she would be tortured and put to death; friends gathered around her, imploring her not to go on directly in the face of danger and death .[12]

In spite of the warnings, after her visit to Boston and a brief trip to Auburn, she traveled throughout New England in the spring of 1859, doing "missionary" work. She met with Brown several times, once suggesting to him that July 4 would be an ideal time for his raids to begin. While Brown gathered guns and sent his sons to the South to rent a farmhouse near Harpers Ferry, Virginia, Harriet continued trying to recruit men and to raise funds for the liberating strike.

Her "missionary" work also included influencing men such as Seward who were in positions of power and speaking to Northern audiences. Vigilance committees in New England were more involved in fundraising and propaganda than they were in direct aid to fugitives. Their source of propaganda came from accounts by fugitives themselves, which "produced a great effect on all who heard them." Harriet was never a paid speaker like Douglass and Sojourner Truth, but she appeared on the speakers' platform at various meetings and conventions.

"For eight or ten years previous to the breaking out of the Rebellion," wrote William Wells Brown,

> *all who frequented anti-slavery conventions, lectures, picnics, and fairs could not fail to have seen a black woman of medium size, upper front teeth gone, smiling countenance, attired in coarse, but neat apparel, with an old-fashioned reticule or bag suspended by her side . . . and who, on taking her seat, would at once drop off into a sound sleep.*[13]

Appearances could be deceiving. There is no complete record of any of her speeches, but the *Liberator* published an incomplete account of Harriet's appearance in Framingham, Massachusetts, on July 4, 1859. She was introduced by Higginson, the president of the Massachusetts Anti-Slavery Society, to a crowd of thousands gathered outdoors. Harriet was usually introduced as Moses or "our foster sister Moses," partly to protect her identity, since Maryland could have demanded of Massachusetts its right to have her returned under the Fugitive Slave Law.

" 'Moses,' the deliverer, then stood up before the au-

83

dience, who greeted her with enthusiastic cheers," recorded the secretary, James Yerrington.

She spoke briefly, telling the story of her sufferings as a slave, her escape, and her achievements on the Underground Railroad, in a style of quaint simplicity, which excited the most profound interest in her hearers.

"The mere words could do no justice to the speaker," he went on, "and therefore we do not undertake to give them; but we advise all our readers to take the earliest opportunity to see and hear her."[14]

Another account says that when Harriet spoke, she used rolling words that were colorful and biting. She often told a parable to make her points. She was emphatically opposed to colonization, that is, the suggestion that freed slaves should be returned to the colony of Liberia in Africa. At the New England Colored Citizens' Convention in August she told a story of a man who had sowed onions and garlic on his land to increase his dairy production. He soon found, however, that his butter was strong and would not sell, so he decided to sow clover instead, but the wind had blown the onions and garlic all over his field.

Just so, the white people had got the Negroes here to do their drudgery, Harriet said, and now they were trying to root them out and ship them to Africa. "But, they can't do it; we're rooted here, and they can't pull us up."[15]

As Harriet was speaking in July and August of 1859, John Brown was in Virginia, preparing to raid the federal arsenal at Harpers Ferry. Once successful in seizing arms from the arsenal, Brown expected slaves to flee from their masters and to join him in the mountains. July 4 passed, and Brown sent his son to find Harriet Tubman and the recruits she had promised, but Harriet had mysteriously dropped from sight. "With Maryland slaveholders clamoring for her head and Brown's supporters frantically trying to find "the woman," the tireless general had fallen ill. Her abolitionist

*John Brown changed the course of history
with his raid on Harpers Ferry.*

work and labor to support her parents had resulted in exhaustion. She lay in a New Bedford, Massachusetts, cottage for weeks, sunk in sleeping spells, too weak to sit up and even to think when she was awake.

In mid-September, Lewis Hayden, a black supporter of Brown's, discovered her whereabouts and sent her an urgent message, "Come to Boston at once." On her way to join Brown, she had gone as far as New York City when she sensed that something was wrong. She could not tell what at first, but finally she told her hostess that Captain Brown must be in trouble. The next day's newspaper told of the failed raid on Harpers Ferry and Brown's capture by federal troops. When she learned that Brown's two sons had died in the raid, Harriet suddenly understood the significance of the two heads beside Brown's in her dream. She had not been able to save the old man, after all.

9
IRREPRESSIBLE CONFLICT

John Brown and eighteen men, including five blacks, seized the arsenal at Harpers Ferry, Virginia, for a day and took prominent townspeople as hostages. Federal troops were called in to dislodge them, and all but four of Brown's men were killed or wounded and later hanged. Brown himself was captured, tried for treason, and hanged in December. His papers and letters, with names of his supporters, were confiscated from the farmhouse from which he had launched the raid.

Brown's action ignited the smoldering controversy between the North and the South. Many Northerners saw Brown as a martyr to the antislavery cause, but Southerners were outraged that the North would arm black men and send them to the South to free slaves. They demanded to know who had given Brown rifles and accused Northern abolitionists of supporting him, not an unreasonable charge.

Harriet had no small part in lighting the fire. Although she was not at Harpers Ferry, she had freed a hundred slaves by 1860 and had encouraged many more to flee; she had spoken out to arouse abolitionist sentiment in the North; she had recruited men and raised money for Brown among exiles in Canada and in New England cities, and she had been an inspiration to him. She believed that the raid would have a powerful effect, whether it was successful or not, by attracting the country's attention to the issue of slavery.

Brown's action and subsequent execution certainly attracted the attention of the country, so much so that Douglass and three of the Secret Six fled to Canada as soon as they heard of the raid. Harriet was whisked off, too, for a time. Through newspaper and congressional investigations in 1859 and 1860, it became clear that she was a co-conspirator, "the woman" Brown mentioned in his letters and papers.

To Harriet, John Brown was a hero and martyr. She spoke of him with reverence for the rest of her life as "John Brown, my dearest friend." "It was not John Brown that died at Charleston," she said, "it was Christ—the savior of our people."[1] Among white men, she regarded Brown, not Abraham Lincoln, as the true emancipator of the slaves.

The year following Brown's execution, mob spirits reigned in the principal cities of the North and South. Vigorous attempts were made to repress blacks; new military companies began forming in all parts of Maryland. Underground Railroad records were destroyed or hidden, lest they fall into the hands of a proslavery mob. William Still purposely omitted important details in the escape stories of fugitives he interviewed and kept records on loose slips of paper instead.

In such times, Harriet was advised to lie low. After the John Brown affair, she was too well known and too hated to work successfully for the underground. She rested for a while in Auburn, but Harriet could never stay quiet for long. She emerged one April day in 1860 in a fury when slaveholders tried to recapture a fugitive slave in Troy, New York.

Harriet was in Troy, staying with a relative and on her way to attend an antislavery meeting in Boston when news came to the black community that a fugitive slave had been seized and was to come up before a U.S. commissioner for a hearing on his freedom. Charles Nalle was a very light-skinned man who had escaped from Culpepper County, Virginia, two years before to join his wife. Nalle was an octoroon, meaning that he was one-eighth black. His father was his white master; his slave mother was a quadroon, one-quarter black. The agent sent to reclaim him was actually his younger half brother.[2]

As soon as Harriet knew of the hearing, she started for the commissioner's office, "scattering the tidings as she went." An excited crowd gathered around the office at First and State streets. A wagon was waiting to carry Nalle off, but the crowd was already so big that the officers did not dare bring him down. Harriet forced her way through the crowd and upstairs to the door of the room where Nalle was. She positioned herself near a window so that her sunbonnet could be seen by the crowd below. As long as they could see her there, they felt sure that Nalle had not been taken out another way. At one point she sent out some little boys to cry, "Fire!" Bells rang, and the crowd increased in size.

"The crowd at this time numbered nearly a thousand persons," wrote the *Troy Whig*. "Many of them were black, and a good share were of the female sex. They blocked up State Street from First Street to the alley, and kept surging to and fro."[3]

When the officers tried to clear the stairs, Harriet assumed one of her favorite poses, that of a harmless old woman. "Come, old woman, you must get out of this," said one of the officers; "I must have the way cleared; if you can't get down alone, someone will help you." Acting even more decrepit, Harriet twitched and moved away from him, keeping her place.

Finally, Nalle was brought out, "a tall, handsome, intelligent *white* man with his wrists manacled together, walking between the U.S. marshal and another officer—behind him his brother and his master—so like him that one could

89

hardly be told from the other.'' Nalle's attorney had secured an appeal before a judge of the state supreme court, and he was to be taken there.

Harriet decided, however, not to wait for the courts. She roused from her stooping posture, threw up a window, and cried to the crowd: ''Here he comes—take him!''

What ensued was a mob action with Harriet in the lead. She grabbed one of the officers and pulled him away from Nalle, then she grabbed the other. With her arms in a fierce grip around Nalle, she called to the crowd to go to the river. They were knocked down again and again, beaten with policemen's clubs, the slave helpless in his manacles. Harriet's clothes and even her shoes were pulled from her, but she hung on and cheered the crowd with her voice until they reached the river and Nalle was put in a boat. Harriet and part of the crowd followed on a ferry.

The telegraph preceded them, however, and Nalle was seized on the other side. Amid gunfire, which resulted in the wounding of two men, the crowd rescued Nalle again from the third floor of a building, with Harriet actually carrying him in her arms. Persuading a man passing by with a horse and wagon to help, Harriet loaded Nalle into the wagon for a quick ride west.[4]

Harriet went back into hiding then as her name appeared in the headlines. Nalle returned to Troy a few months later, after the community raised funds to buy his freedom from his master. A plaque placed on a bank building in 1908 commemorates the spot where the city's citizens prevented the return of one of their own to slavery. ''In this rescue, a colored woman was prominent,'' an antislavery pamphlet recounted, ''a woman known extensively among the colored people as Moses.''[5]

Such incidents heightened the hostility between North and South, especially when Southerners were injured in the process of trying to retrieve their ''property.'' The cumulative impact of the Underground Railroad, the testimony of fugitive slaves, John Brown's raid, and the Fugitive Slave Law made slavery an issue that no one could avoid. William

Seward described the free-labor system of the North and the slave-labor system of the South as an "irrepressible conflict between opposing and enduring forces."[6]

In May Harriet emerged from hiding and continued on her way to the New England Anti-Slavery Society Conference. Franklin Sanborn squired her around to the homes of eminent Bostonians and to Concord, where she was a popular guest in the "antislavery parlors" of the Lowells, Emersons, Alcotts, and Manns. There she finally found the kind white women she had dreamed of as a youth.

After listening to one distinguished speaker after another at the antislavery conference, Harriet remained in Boston for a women's suffrage meeting on June 1. Women's rights and black rights were linked in the minds of feminists such as Elizabeth Cady Stanton: "For white man is born to do whatever he can, for the woman and the Negro there is no such privilege."[7]

Harriet spoke at the suffrage meeting, telling the story of her adventures "in a modest, but quaint and amusing style which won much applause."[8] The famous novelist Louisa May Alcott (author of *Little Women*) was profoundly stirred by Harriet's courage.

Her words won no applause, however, from the proslavery writer John Bell Robinson, who said her kind of work was treason and made secession inevitable. He wrote:

> *"What could be more insulting after having lost over $50,000 worth of property by that deluded negress, than for a large congregation of whites and well-educated people of Boston to endorse such an imposition on the Constitutional rights of the slave States."* They were worshipping *"the goddess of liberty in the shape of a poor deluded Negro woman."*[9]

Rhetoric continued on both sides through the summer of 1860. William Seward was hoping to become the presidential nominee of the Republican party, but proslavery forces attacked him bitterly for his abolitionist views, his alleged support of John Brown, and his friendship with Harriet Tubman. In an effort to gain broader support, Seward made the public statement that the hanging of Brown was "necessary and just," but that lost him the support of Wendell Phillips and the antislavery radicals. When the Republicans met in the summer of 1860 to choose their candidate, the lesser known Abraham Lincoln was selected on the third ballot. With Democrats split on the slavery issue, Lincoln became the favored candidate, but his election would be unacceptable to the South.

Events were moving toward civil war, so Harriet made one last attempt to free her sister. Returning to Maryland in December 1860, she found that her sister had died. She brought out a party of seven instead.

"I write to let thee know that Harriet Tubman is again in these parts," Thomas Garrett wrote to Still on December 1.

> *She arrived last evening from one of her trips of mercy to God's poor, bringing two men with her as far as New Castle. . . . the wife of one of the men, with two or three children, was left some thirty miles below and I gave Harriet ten dollars to hire a man with a carriage to take them to Chester County. She said a man offered for the sum to bring them on. I shall be very uneasy about them, till I hear they are safe. There is now much more risk on the road, till they arrive here, than there has been for several months past, as we find that some poor, worthless wretches [people hoping to collect rewards] are constantly on the look out on two roads that they cannot well avoid more especially with carriages, yet as it is Harriet who seems to have had a special angel to guard her on her journey of mercy, I have hope.* [10]

Still's book noted the group was the last Harriet piloted and that they came through "great tribulation." [11]

During the last months before the "irrepressible conflict" broke out, Harriet sensed that war was coming. There was no turning back from the collision course she and others had set when Abraham Lincoln was elected in November 1860. Last-minute compromises were presented to the Senate, including one that called for the return of fugitive slaves and the prosecution of slave conductors. Much against her will, Harriet was hurried off again to Canada, in fear that she might be traded off to the South in a mad effort to buy peace. All to no avail. "They may say, 'Peace! Peace!' as much as they like," Harriet told Sanborn. "I know there's going to be war!"[12]

10
BEHIND THE LINES

Even before Abraham Lincoln was inaugurated, in March 1861, South Carolina seceded from the Union. Ten more states followed, and the Confederate States of America were formed. A month after the new president took office, the Confederacy attacked Fort Sumter, the federal fort in the Charleston harbor, and the Civil War began.

Harriet wanted to be part of the action. For her, for other blacks both enslaved and free, and for abolitionists in the North, the war continued the moral crusade against the evil of slavery. "Now I've been free, I know what a dreadful condition slavery is," Harriet Tubman explained.

I have seen hundreds of escaped slaves, but I never saw one who was willing to go back and be a slave. . . . I think slavery is the next thing to hell. If a person would send another into bondage, he would, it appears to me, be bad enough to send him into hell, if he could.

94

She did not blame the slaveholders individually for this.

They don't know any better, it's the way they were brought up; "Make the little slaves mind you, or flog them," was what they said to their children, and they were brought up with the whip in their hands. Now that wasn't the way on all plantations; there were good masters and mistresses, as I've heard tell, but I didn't happen to come across any of them.[1]

Harriet had foreseen the day when all her people would be free from the evil of slavery. Three years before, when she had been staying with the Reverend Henry Highland Garnet in New York City, a vision of emancipation came to her in the night. She woke up singing, "My people are free! My people are free!"

"Oh Harriet, you've come to torment us before the time," Reverend Garnet admonished, saying that he thought his grandchildren might see emancipation but he never would. Harriet persisted, saying that he would see the day of freedom and see it soon.[2]

Always one to turn dreams into action, Harriet Tubman hurried down from Canada in the spring of 1861 to join the war effort. The woman John Brown had dubbed *General* may have seemed a likely recruit to some, but first she had to convince someone in power that a short black woman of forty belonged in the Union Army.

Through her New England abolitionist friends, Harriet obtained an interview with the governor of Massachusetts, John A. Andrew. Andrew hated slavery and had defended John Brown's moral position after the Harpers Ferry raid: "Whatever may be thought of John Brown's acts," he said, "John Brown himself was right."[3] Andrew was the first governor to send a regiment to fight in the Union Army.

Andrew agreed to send Harriet to South Carolina, where the Union Army had captured the islands off the coast and

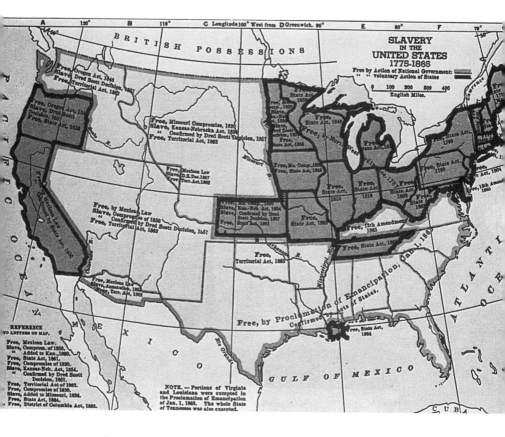

*Some states chose to abolish slavery while others were
forced by the government to free the slaves.*

instituted a blockade of Charleston Harbor. When the Yankees established camp on the islands, plantation owners and
the white population fled to the mainland, but most of their
slaves stayed. Other slaves from the mainland began fleeing
to the Union lines.

At first the army did not know what to do with the
escaped slaves. A few were actually returned to their owners before General Benjamin F. Butler said they should be

"contraband of war" (seized war material). As "contraband," they were put to work in the Union cause. Northern soldiers knew very little of slavery and slaves, however, and someone was needed to act as a liaison.

Harriet was impatient to go. Indeed, there is some indication that she had already followed the Union Army into Maryland in the spring of 1861, leading slaves there to federal lines. When the islands off South Carolina were captured in November and December, Harriet made a quick visit home to Auburn to ask abolitionists there to look after her parents; then she hurried back to Boston. A party was given in honor of her anticipated departure at the Twelfth Baptist Church in February 1862, and she finally left in May on a government transport. Her orders were to report to General David Hunter at the Hilton Head headquarters of the Army of the South. Despite the delays, Harriet was probably the first woman, black or white, to go to the battlefront.

Beaufort, the biggest town on the islands, was bustling with government agents, Union soldiers, and "missionaries" from the North who had come to help the contrabands. Harriet began at once to work with "her people," even though she could hardly understand the dialect of the Carolina blacks. "Why, their language down there in the far South is just as different from ours in Maryland as you can think," she said. "They laughed when they heard me talk, and I could not understand them."[4]

She could understand their needs. In a letter dictated to her friend Franklin Sanborn, she said, "Among other duties which I have, is that of looking after the hospital here for contrabands. Most of those coming from the mainland are very destitute, almost naked. I am trying to find places for those able to work, and provide for them as best I can, so as to lighten the burden of the Government as much as possible, while at the same time they learn to respect themselves by earning their own living."[5] With the first and only pay she received from the government during the war—two hundred dollars—Harriet built a washhouse where she could teach the women how to do laundry for the soldiers and to earn their own living.

Harriet was entitled to draw Army rations, but she did not want to arouse jealousy among the destitute ex-slaves. Instead she supported herself by making root beer, gingerbread, and pies at night, paying someone to peddle the food through the camps during the day while she worked.

The military task of the Department of the South was to hold and blockade the southern coast from Charleston, South Carolina, to Jacksonville, Florida, to try to force Charleston to surrender, and to harass the Confederates inland. Part of that harassment included the tactic of "capturing" or "welcoming" blacks behind the Union lines, thus weakening the economy of the Confederacy. Small raiding parties were sent upriver from the coast to destroy property and capture slaves, arms, and food.

Enough blacks were recruited from the contrabands to fill two regiments of a thousand soldiers each, but President Lincoln hesitated to use them. He didn't want to offend the slaveholding border states of Maryland and Kentucky, which had not yet joined the Confederacy. Frederick Douglass, however, kept advocating the use of a "strong black arm," and when it became obvious that things were not going well for the North, Lincoln's hesitation ended. In the late fall of 1862, the New England abolitionist minister Thomas Higginson arrived at Camp Saxton, a few miles from Beaufort, to recruit and train the first black regiment in the Union Army, the First South Carolina Volunteers.

From his tent by the Salkahatchie River, Higginson wrote to his wife,

Who should drive out to see me today but Harriet Tubman who is living at Beaufort as a sort of nurse and general care taker; she sends her regards to you. . . . I wish you could see how pretty our encampment looks with its 250 tents glimmering in the moonlight. . . .[6]

The First South Carolina Volunteers became valued
members of the Union Army's forces.

Colonel James Montgomery, who had been with John Brown in Kansas, came to train the Second South Carolina Volunteers. Harriet welcomed both officers and worked closely with the regiments. Camp Saxton was a joyful scene when the regiments and camp followers gathered on January 1, 1863, to hear the reading of Lincoln's Emancipation Proclamation, granting freedom to all slaves in the Confederacy. Governor Andrew sent down copies of the proclamation, and the camp celebrated with a grand barbecue and jubilee.

When she reported to General Hunter, Harriet was first assigned to work for surgeon Henry Durrant at the Contraband Hospital as a nurse. For those first few months, she was a utility worker, going wherever she was needed, from the Carolinas to Florida, nursing soldiers and contrabands alike, bathing fevers, dressing wounds, and delivering babies.

Besides nursing and acting as a liaison, Harriet had been recommended by Governor Andrew as a valuable person to gather information about the rebels' positions inland. Black women were especially good at slipping in and out of the Confederate lines and going from plantation to plantation because they were assumed to be slaves. Harriet herself was a natural at spying. She could use her nondescript appearance and underground connections to travel easily behind the lines. Besides her talent for concealment, she never forgot any detail of a route she had taken. Harriet also had a keen sense of people; "She could look at you and tell whether you could be trusted."[7]

In the third year of the war, in 1863, Harriet Tubman was called on to organize a scouting service. She picked seven former slaves who knew the inland areas and the location of food storage areas and rebel ammunition dumps, and she recruited two black river pilots who knew the rivers that Union gunboats could follow in from the coast.[8] In effect Harriet was in charge of an intelligence service, under the directions and orders of several generals and the secretary of war, Edwin Stanton. Her scouts surveyed the countryside

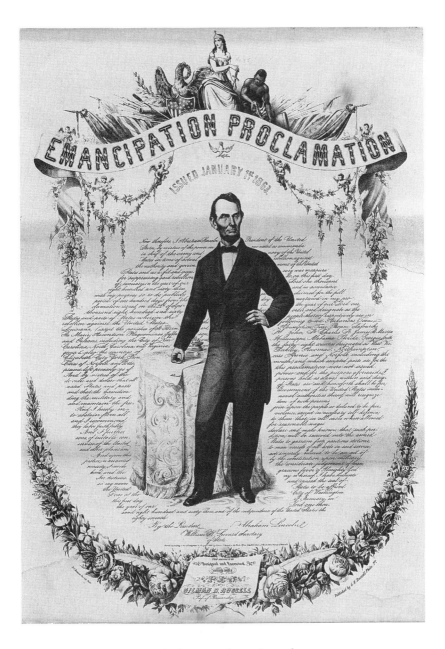

*A decorated version of
the Emancipation Proclamation*

in preparation for a series of raids led by Higginson and Montgomery.

On the first raid, in January, Higginson's black regiment went up the St. Mary's River, which divides Georgia from Florida. They encountered rebel fire but brought back large quantities of railroad iron, lumber, bricks, rice, and a herd of sheep. Then, in February, the regiment went up the St. John's River in Florida. One of the purposes of the raids was to gain recruits for Montgomery's regiment (the Second South Carolina Volunteers), which was not yet full.

"I have reliable information that there are large numbers of able-bodied Negroes in that vicinity who are watching for an opportunity to join us," General Rufus Saxton wrote to Secretary of War Stanton on March 6.[9] (Saxton's "reliable information" came from Harriet's spies.) Four days later the two regiments went up the St. John's and captured Jacksonville; then Montgomery raided farther up-river to Palatka. Some slaves were recruited, but still more were needed. On the next raid, Harriet would go, too.

From her quiet start as nurse and liaison, Harriet was becoming a valuable military aide. Among blacks, her reputation carried over from her underground days. "When the Negro put on the 'blue,' " wrote William Wells Brown,

"Moses" was in her glory and travelled from camp to camp, being always treated in the most respectful manner. The black men would have died for this woman, for they believed that she had a charmed life.[10]

Her leadership abilities were confirmed on her most famous raid up the Combahee River in June. Harriet's scouts had learned from slaves on plantations along the river's banks the location of Confederate torpedoes in the rivers. When she reported this information to General Hunter, he asked if she would like to go with several gunboats to take up the torpedoes, to destroy railroads and bridges, to cut off supplies from the rebel troops, and to collect slaves. She said she would go if Colonel Montgomery was appointed commander of the expedition.

Three Yankee gunboats steamed up the Combahee, meeting little opposition—one Confederate soldier was killed—and successfully avoiding the torpedoes. Confirming the good advance work, a Confederate investigating officer wrote,

> *The enemy seems to have been well posted as to the character and capacity of our troops and their small chance of encountering opposition, and to have been well guided by persons thoroughly acquainted with the river and country.*[11]

As the raiding party advanced, burning crops and buildings, hundreds of slaves fled from plantations along the river's banks to "Lincoln's gunboats."

"I never saw such a sight," Harriet recalled.

> *We laughed and laughed and laughed. Here you'd see a woman with a pail on her head, rice a-smoking in it just as she'd taken it from the fire, young one hanging on behind, one hand around her forehead to hold on, the other hand digging into the rice pot, eating with all its might; a-hold of her dress two or three more; down her back a bag with a pig in it. . . . Sometimes the women would come with twins hanging around the necks; it appears I never saw so many twins in my life; bags on their shoulders, baskets on their heads and young ones tagging behind, all loaded; pigs squealing, chickens screaming, young ones squealing.*[12]

Colonel Montgomery became concerned about delays in loading. He called on Harriet to "give 'em a song." With great emotional fervor, she poured out a melody with improvised words meant to calm and reassure those slaves whose masters had told them the Yankees had horns:

103

Of all the whole creation in the East or in the West,
The glorious Yankee nation is the greatest and the best!
Come along! Come along! Don't be alarmed,
Uncle Sam's rich enough to give us all a farm!

Come along! Come along! Don't be a fool,
Uncle Sam's rich enough to send us all to school!'', etc.

As she chanted the refrain "Come along!", Harriet raised her arms with an imperious gesture and the crowd responded with shouts of "Glory! Glory!" Seven hundred and fifty-six slaves were taken on board.

The whole raid was recounted by a Wisconsin journalist who gave Harriet full credit for leading it. His dispatch appeared on the front page of the *New York Herald*: "Colonel Montgomery and his gallant band of three hundred black soldiers, under the guidance of a black woman, dashed into the enemy's country, struck a bold and effective blow. . . ." At the celebration in Beaufort, he wrote, "the Colonel was followed by a speech from the black woman, who led the raid and under whose inspiration it was originated and conducted."[13] If the account is correct, the Combahee raid may have been the only military engagement in American history led by a woman. She certainly gained the respect of the Union officers, who gave her the title *General* and never failed to tip their caps when meeting her.

Glory had an impractical side. Shortly after the Combahee raid, Harriet dictated a letter to Sanborn explaining that

> *On our late expedition up the Combahee River, in coming on board the boat, I was carrying two pigs for a poor sick woman, who had a child to carry, and the order "double quick" was given, and I started to run, stepped on my dress, it being rather long, and fell and tore it almost off, so that when I got on board the boat, there was hardly anything left of it but shreds. I made up my mind then I would*

never wear a long dress on another expedition of the kind, but would have a bloomer as soon as I could get it.[14]

When she got it, Harriet's military uniform consisted of a coat and dress in federal blue with a large bandanna to be worn over her short hair. She carried a satchel filled with first-aid equipment, her musket, and a canteen. On expeditions, she wore the bloomers, a fact of which she was proud in the heady days of women's rights after the war.

Nearly all the able-bodied men brought out in the Combahee raid joined the black South Carolina regiments, which now numbered four. As Higginson and Montgomery were leading their regiments on raids in May, the first regiment of black troops from the North came down to Beaufort. They were the Fifty-fourth Massachusetts Infantry, which included two sons of Frederick Douglass and was led by Colonel Robert Shaw. As she had worked closely with Higginson, Montgomery, and the First and Second South Carolina Volunteers, Harriet welcomed the regiments recruited by Governor Andrew and Douglass and stayed with them, cooking, doing laundry, and carrying dispatches.

Except for the raids, the black regiments had not been tried in full-fledged battle, and they were eager to prove their mettle and their loyalty to the Union. The Fifty-fourth was chosen to lead a frontal assault on the rebel-held Fort Wagner, which stood on Morris Island and blocked the entrance to Charleston Harbor. Before Colonel Shaw led the Fifty-fourth into the attack, Harriet served him his last meal and had a vision of his death.

The fort could be approached only over a narrow, almost mile-long causeway, with a salt marsh on one side and the sea on the other. After participating in a diversionary attack on a nearby island, the Fifty-fourth was transported to Morris Island on July 18 and placed in the front of combined black and white forces. After a day of artillery bombardment, the march to the fort began in the evening, the sounds of battle accompanied by a thunderstorm. Shaw led his men over a ditch and up to the parapet of the fort in the face of heavy musket fire from the defenders. There he was killed. Fifteen hundred Union soldiers were killed, wounded, captured, or reported missing. The battle was lost, but the black troops proved their bravery with their lives.

Harriet helped bury the dead and nurse the wounded. The battle, and the beach crowded with casualties, left a vivid impression on her mind, which she described to the historian, Thomas Hart Benton:

> And then we saw the lightning, and that was the guns; and then we heard the thunder, and that was the big guns; and then we heard the rain falling, and that was the drops of blood falling; and when we came to get in the crops, it was dead men that we reaped.[15]

11
THE NATION'S WOUNDS

Weary from her months of scouting, raiding, and nursing, Harriet thought of going back north.

"I have now been absent two years almost and have just got letters from my friends in Auburn, urging me to come home," she wrote to Franklin Sanborn in June 1863. "My father and mother are old and in feeble health and need my care and attention." But that summer she still had important work to do for the Union army, and she felt she could not leave. "I shall be sure to come and see you if I live to go North."[1]

Harriet lived, but after nursing the men wounded in the terrible assault on Fort Wagner, she herself needed a rest. Lincoln had finally found a general who would fight— General Ulysses S. Grant—and with thousands of new men on the lines, the North was winning. So, in the spring of 1864, Harriet requested a leave of absence. She would not return to the war until only nursing was needed.

Once she was home in Auburn, total exhaustion took over; her sleeping spells became more frequent. As she took care of her parents, the leading citizens of the town took care of her, too, bringing food to the door. One visitor was

Sarah Hopkins Bradford, daughter of a professor at the Auburn Theological Seminary. Bradford had looked after Ben and Rit, writing the letters asking when Harriet would come back. Now, as Harriet rested, Bradford sat and listened to her stories. These stories would go into a biography called *Scenes in the Life of Harriet Tubman,* the first of many books and articles telling of her experiences.

In a few months Harriet was well enough to travel. Whenever she felt this yen, she just went to the local station and waited for the first train going in the right direction. She headed to Boston where she met another black heroine of the day, Sojourner Truth. Tall and rangy, Sojourner had been born a slave in New York State, when slavery was still legal there. She knew hard labor, but she had successfully sued for her freedom. As a free woman, she became a speaker for religion, women's rights, and abolition. That summer of 1864 she was on her way to an audience with the president.

Harriet didn't much like Lincoln. He had been too slow to emancipate the slaves, she thought, and too willing to pay black soldiers less than white soldiers.

You see we colored people didn't understand then that he was our friend. All we knew was that the first colored troops sent South from Massachusetts only got seven dollars a month, while the white got fifteen. We didn't like that.[2]

Early in the war, Harriet had criticized Lincoln for his slowness to act. The writer Lydia Maria Child recounted her rough words:

She talks politics sometimes, and her uncouth utterance is wiser than the plans of politicians. She said the other day: "They may send the flower of their young men down South, to die of the fever in the summer and the ague in the winter (For 'tis cold down there, though 'tis down South). They may send them one year, two year, three year, till they tire of sending or till they use up the young men. All of no use. God is ahead of Mister Lincoln. God won't let Mister Lincoln beat the South till he does the right thing. Mister Lincoln, he is a great man, and I'm a poor nigger, but this nigger can tell Mister Lincoln how to save the money and the young men. He can do it by setting the Negroes free.[3]

Sojourner, sixty-seven years old when she and Harriet met, was more patient with the president. "It takes a great while to turn about this great ship of state," she told Harriet, who listened unconvinced.[4] It was Sojourner Truth who, in her interview that fall, thanked the president for what he had done for her people. Harriet had no wish to meet President Lincoln, so whenever she went to Washington and wanted a powerful man's ear, she talked to her friend William Seward, who was secretary of state.

As Harriet restored her health and her spirits by visiting friends, the Union General William T. Sherman marched into Atlanta and on through Georgia to the sea, cutting the Confederacy in half. In January of 1865 he turned north to the Confederate capital, Richmond. By the time Harriet headed for Washington to collect a pass for army transportation back to Hilton Head, the war was almost over.

Also in Washington that winter was the prominent black physician and abolitionist, Martin R. Delany, and Harriet was briefly enlisted in an ambitious plan. Delany had been urging Lincoln to create a black army under black officers that would go south and recruit slaves. The slaves could be prepared for the arrival of the army, he said, through the Underground Railroad, "a system of communication known to Negroes," and with the support of Harriet Tubman. Delany argued so persuasively that he received a commission as the first Negro major in American history. His next step was to enlist Harriet Tubman, who agreed to do the advance work.

Before she could leave, however, national events overtook Delany's campaign. On March 4, Lincoln gave his

109

Harriet was not one of President Abraham Lincoln's greatest fans. She felt he took much too long to free the slaves.

Second Inaugural Address, urging "malice toward none and charity for all" in finishing the "work we are in" and binding up "the nation's wounds." Harriet's pass to Hilton Head was dated March 20, but on April 9, the South, under its heroic general Robert E. Lee, surrendered. Five days later the president Harriet had never met was fatally shot in his box at the Ford Theater. Secretary of State Seward was also shot that fateful night, but he recovered.

No longer needed on the military front, Harriet was persuaded by some members of the Sanitary Commission to work in the government hospitals at Fort Monroe, Virginia, bringing her valuable nursing skills to some of the war's last casualties. Much of Harriet's work as a nurse at the beginning of the war had been routine. The contrabands she cared for in South Carolina were mainly suffering from malnutrition after weeks of hiding out in the woods and swamps. Even when she began treating wounded soldiers in hospitals, there was little she could do but try to make them more comfortable and keep them clean.

I'd go to the hospital early every morning. I'd get a big chunk of ice and put it in a basin, and fill it with water; then I'd take a sponge and begin. First man I'd come to, I'd thrash away the flies, and they'd rise, like bees around a hive. Then I'd begin to bathe their wounds, and by the time I'd bathed off three or four the fire and heat would have melted the ice and made the water warm, and it would be as red as clear blood. Then I'd go and get more in, and by the time I got to the next one, the flies would be around the first ones black and thick as ever.[5]

In such unsanitary conditions, dysentery was rampant, and the doctors had no medicine to treat the disorder, whose primary symptom is severe, painful diarrhea. Drawing on slave knowledge of herbal remedies, Harriet concocted her own. At night she collected the roots of a pond lily and parts of a wild geranium called cranesbill. Then she beat the plants to a powder and mixed them with water, brewing a tea. She gave the brew to black and white soldiers alike, and it improved their health in a day.[6] Because of her success, she was sent to Fernandina, Florida, to treat men ''dying off like sheep'' from dysentery.

Harriet acquired a reputation for having unusual healing power, a miracle woman, the soldiers said, whose mere touch could heal the sick. Surgeon Henry Durrant was willing to share with her the little ''medicine'' the army had. ''Will Capt. Warfield please let 'Moses' have a little Bourbon whisky for medicinal purposes,'' Durrant wrote to the commissary representative.[7] Whiskey was used as a sedative.

Wartime nursing was not limited to loving care, healing teas, and a shot of whiskey. Pure physical strength and a strong stomach were also required. Harriet told of assisting at a leg amputation where she held down a man who bit through the lead bullet placed in his mouth.

Conditions in the hospitals at Fort Monroe were even worse than what Harriet had seen earlier. Alarmed by serious abuses there, she went back to Washington in July 1865 to complain to the surgeon general, who directed that she be appointed a matron, or superintendent. She returned to the hospitals on a government transport, but it appears the appointment as matron did not materialize or that she was unable to make improvements. Like many other veterans, she realized that her mission was finished. She saw no further use for her talents.

All through the war, Harriet had received no pay, other than the two hundred dollars she used to build a washhouse. As the country moved on to peacetime tasks, she belatedly understood the importance of securing some compensation. Assorted passes confirmed the official sanction for her work, and she collected a few letters, attesting to her service.

''I certify that I have been acquainted with Harriet Tubman for nearly two years,'' Surgeon Durrant wrote in 1864,

and my position . . . has given me frequent and ample opportunity to observe her general deport-

Harriet Tubman was more than an ex-slave turned abolitionist. She was also a nurse and a spy for the Union Army.

ment, particularly her kindness and attention to the sick and suffering of her own race. I take much pleasure in testifying to the esteem in which she is generally held.

"I wish to commend to your attention, Mrs. Harriet Tubman, a most remarkable woman, and invaluable as a scout. I have been acquainted with her character and actions for several years," Colonel Montgomery had written to General Gilmore in 1863. General Saxton signed an endorsement on the back: "I approve of Colonel Montgomery's estimate of the value of Harriet Tubman's services."[8]

But these letters were recommendations, not commissions, and the country was not in the habit of paying blacks for unofficial work, much less paying them adequately. When the black regiments were told they would receive half the pay of white soldiers, the men decided to accept no pay at all until the authorities came around to paying them equally. A black woman's right to military pay seemed beyond consideration.

Tired and penniless, Moses headed home with a pocketful of letters testifying to her heroism and service. She boarded a northbound train, carrying a pass that entitled her to half fare as a government employee. The conductor refused to believe, however, that this poor, black woman could be entitled to half fare. Insulting her, he ordered her to leave the passenger car. When she firmly stood her ground, the conductor asked three men to help. Together they shoved her into the baggage car, where she rode for the rest of the trip, her arm and shoulder badly wrenched.

News of the incident appeared in abolitionist newspapers, which commented that the struggle for black rights would continue. Harriet Tubman had spent the prime of her life in this struggle. Now old beyond her forty-five years, she bore the physical bruise from the shove and the spiritual wound from the insult home to years of poverty and an insecure freedom.

12
OL' CHARIOT

In the defeated South after the Civil War, ex-slaves tried out their new freedom. But even in states like Maryland that had not joined the rebellion, blacks had to walk a fine line among whites, as John Tubman discovered one autumn afternoon in 1867 on a road in Dorchester County. He and a white man, Robert Vincent, had quarreled early in the day over some ashes, strange as it may seem. During the quarrel, Vincent had threatened to kill Tubman and chased him away with an ax. Meeting Tubman again on the road that afternoon, Vincent asked him if "he was the same man as he was in the morning."

"Yes," the black man responded, perhaps with a hint of boldness in his voice. Vincent drove on about 40 yards (36 m) in his wagon, reached for his gun, turned around, and fired deliberately at Tubman, who fell to the ground. Continuing on his way, Vincent never even stopped to see whether his shot had been fatal. Later that fall he was indicted and tried for murder, but a jury found him not guilty. The only witness to the shooting was Tubman's thirteen-year-old son, who had been standing in the woods near the roadside.[1]

In the victorious North, black lives seemed more secure. From a distance, Harriet Tubman plunged eagerly into the work of Reconstruction by trying to raise money for two freedmen's schools in North Carolina. She asked for contributions from her wealthy abolitionist friends, borrowed money where she could, addressed public meetings, and gave parties to raise funds, which she sent to the schools. But gradually over the next forty-five years of her especially long life, her struggle became more personal.

She underwent an operation in an unsuccessful attempt to relieve the pressure on her brain from her head injury of long ago. Offered an anesthetic, she asked only for a bullet to bite and lay motionless during the surgery, mumbling prayers through her clenched teeth.

Friends renewed the attempt to secure back pay for her service during the war. Harriet felt she was entitled to eighteen hundred dollars; she could also have claimed a handsome reward for "recruiting" several hundred black men for the army from the Combahee raid. Despite the backing of men like Seward and letters from generals attesting to her service, Congress took no action.

"You wouldn't think that after I served the flag so faithfully I should come to want in its folds," Harriet Tubman said rather plaintively.[2] While hoping for official recognition, she found ways to support herself. She did a little nursing, a little cooking, a little cleaning and caring for white children; she raised chickens and vegetables and sold them door to door. When times were hard, she would take a bushel basket out to the barn, raise the basket and her voice to God, and ask him to help her fill the basket with food. Often it was the people of Auburn who responded.

Harriet was always short of money because she gave it away to anyone who needed it. She cared for her parents, a brother, William Henry, and grandniece Eva Stewart, whose parents had died in Canada.[3] Mary Ann brought her son Harkless Bowley to stay with Aunt Harriet for a year when the family returned to Maryland from Canada. People who had merely heard of Moses sought out her house, beyond the tollgate on the South Street Road. A friend said the household was "very likely to consist of several old black people, 'bad with the rheumatize,' some forlorn wandering woman, and a couple of children," adding up to as many as twenty people at a time.[4]

She turned no one away. "Long ago when the Lord told me to go free my people," Harriet Tubman recalled,

do you s'pose he wanted me to do this just for a day, or a week? No! The Lord who told me to take care of my people meant me to do it just so long as I live, and so I do what he told me to.[5]

A tall, handsome man named Nelson Davis showed up at the house one day and reminded Harriet that they had met in Port Royal five years before when he was a member of the Eighth U.S. Colored Infantry Volunteers. Townspeople described Davis as "a magnificent physical specimen," about twenty years younger than Harriet, whom he greatly admired.[6] He had been recruited in Philadelphia and served from September 1863 until November 1865, when he was honorably discharged after fighting at Olustee, Boykin's Mill, and Honey Hill. He met Harriet Tubman early in 1864.

Despite his healthy appearance, Davis had tuberculosis and was hardly able to work. Perhaps this weakness aroused Harriet's protective instincts. In the spring of 1869, when she was forty-eight, they were married in the Central Church in Auburn before the first families of the town.

Thereafter Harriet gave her full name as Harriet Tubman Davis. Asked once whether her name should be written with or without the Mrs., Harriet replied, "Anything you like, just so it has the Tubman."[7] That was the name she made famous.

Her name became better known as abolitionist work done in secret before the war became quite public afterward. William Still published his account of the Underground Railroad in 1873. Harriet Tubman's work, too, came to light, as Frederick Douglass said it should:

Most that I have done and suffered in the service of our cause has been in public, and I have received much encouragement at every step of the way. You, on the other hand, have labored in a private way. I have wrought in the day—you in the night. I have had the applause of the crowd and the satisfaction that comes of being approved by the multitude, while the most that you have done has been witnessed by a few trembling, scarred, and footsore bondsmen and women, whom you have led out of the house of bondage, and whose heartfelt "God bless you" has been your only reward.

The midnight sky and the silent stars have been the witnesses of your devotion to freedom and of your heroism. Excepting John Brown—of sacred memory—I know of no one who has willingly encountered more perils and hardships to serve our enslaved people than you have. Much that you have done would seem improbable to those who do not know you as I know you.[8]

Indeed, Harriet Tubman's experiences made a story worth telling. Sarah Bradford decided to help Harriet finish paying the mortgage on her home by writing her biography. She gained promises from Gerrit Smith, Wendell Phillips, and others to pay the cost of printing the book. Then she sat down with Harriet, day after day, listening to her recollections, which she thought were "wonderfully distinct." Bradford wrote to prominent people like Douglass to confirm the stories, but she was quite convinced of their veracity. "No one can hear Harriet talk," she said, "and not believe every word she says."[9] Money from sales of the book was enough to pay off the mortgage, with a little extra.

Harriet Tubman's fame spread, in part, because she was a good storyteller. Writers and reporters who trekked to Auburn for interviews were seldom disappointed.

Moses had no education, yet the most refined person would listen for hours while she related the intensely interesting incidents of her life, told in the simplest manner, but always seasoned with good sense,

wrote William Wells Brown who included her in his book *The Rising Son*. She was "modest and quiet in demeanor," wrote Rosa Belle Holt after an interview for the *Chautauquan*; "a stranger would never guess what depths there are to her nature."[10]

She enjoyed a unique position in Auburn, a one-woman bridge between the black community and well-to-do whites. A grandson of the Hopkins family recalled her visits in an article for the *New Yorker*:

It was always a gala day . . . when Old Harriet Tubman came to call on my grandparents. She would arrive, empty basket suggestively pendent on her arm, having covered the two miles from the small Negro quarter at the other end of Auburn . . . in a swinging half hour or so.

Samuel Hopkins Adams remembered the stories she would tell and the songs she would sing, after a proper amount of coaxing. She

would clap her stringy hands upon her bony knees, rock her powerful frame, snap her eyes, and raise a voice that resounded up to the cupola. It was baritone rather than contralto, that voice, and produced a strangely moving effect of mingled challenge and appeal."[11]

As she sang, she pounded her hands on her knees in time to the rhythm of the old songs of leaving: "Farewell, old master, don't think hard of me. I'm on my way to Canaday, where all the slaves is free" and "When that ole chariot come, I'se gwine to leave you." The slaves had called her that sometimes—"Ol' Chariot"—coming to take them away.

As Harriet reached her sixties and seventies, she had outlived many of her relatives and abolitionist friends. Her parents died in the 1870s. Thomas Garrett died in 1871, and William Seward died a year later. Harriet Tubman would miss his friendship and support. When the home funeral service for "the governor" was over, just before the coffin was to be closed, "a woman black as night stole quietly in," the newspaper account said, "and laying a wreath of field flowers on his feet, as quietly glided out again."[12] As a part of the congregation she also attended the funerals of Wendell Phillips in 1884 and Frederick Douglass in 1895.

Her husband, Nelson Davis, died in 1888 of the tuberculosis that had plagued him. Soon thereafter Congress passed an act giving pensions to widows of Civil War veterans, and Harriet Tubman received a pension of eight dollars a month. In 1898 she resubmitted her own petition for pay for "three years' service as nurse and cook in hospitals and as commander of several men as scouts during the late War of Rebellion." Southern congressmen on the pension committee agreed to increase her widow's pension to twenty dollars a month, in recognition of her service, but they would not grant her a military pension of her own. She was then seventy-eight.

Still, Harriet Tubman did not just sit home and collect her pension. She led in the growth of the African Methodist Episcopal Church in upstate New York, and she went to both A.M.E. and to the white Central Church in Auburn on Sunday mornings. At the biennial conventions of the National Association of Colored Women, she was a familiar figure. She was even invited to England by Queen Victoria to celebrate the Queen's birthday in 1897, but Harriet said

Harriet Tubman in 1895.
She lived a long and eventful life.

she "didn't know enough to go." The Queen sent her a medal as well as a silk shawl to grace the dull-colored dresses she wore, and Harriet kept the Queen's letter, which "was worn to a shadow, so many people read it."[13]

The suffragists of Boston gave a benefit party in her honor in 1897. She had known Susan B. Anthony since her underground days, and she had worked with the women of central New York to gain the right to vote. Asked once if she really believed women should vote, she paused a moment, as if surprised at the question. "I suffered enough to believe it," she quietly replied.[14]

As she aged, Harriet Tubman looked for a way that her houseful of people could be cared for after she died. She dreamed of a home for old, poor, and homeless blacks. With the proceeds from the second edition of her biography, published in 1886, she had a start on the home. She also raised money from the citizens of Auburn, with the support of the mayor and his wife. Then came a break when the twenty-five-acre plot of land next to her own was put up for sale at an auction.

"They was all white folks but me, there, and there I was like a blackberry in a pail of milk, but I hid down in a corner, and no one knew who was bidding. The man began down pretty low, and I kept going up by fifties. At last I got up to fourteen hundred and fifty, and then others stopped bidding, and the man said, 'All done. Who is the buyer?'

" 'Harriet Tubman,' I shouted."[15]

The audience was astonished at this closing bid by an impoverished resident, but Harriet obtained a bank loan with a mortgage on the land, and the Harriet Tubman Home for Aged and Indigent Negroes opened in 1908. She thought the only requirement for admission should be that the applicant have no money, but she had deeded the home to the A.M.E. Zion Church, and the executive board established a one hundred dollar fee. For a time the frame house on an elm-lined street had a matron and a handful of residents, but it did not survive long after Harriet Tubman's death.

Her body shriveled. Her face became furrowed, her hand lost its vigor, and she was confined to a wheelchair with rheumatism. She continued to fall asleep three or four times a day. When awake, however, her mind was astonishingly active, and her memory was sharp. She dictated letters to others, had newspapers read to her, and a songbook, too, so she could memorize the words.

Once in a while there was a flash of the old vigor. The niece she kidnapped, Margaret Stewart, continued living in Auburn as an adult. She and her daughter Alice visited Harriet often and took her sweets. Alice remembered one day when Harriet was feeling like her old self. The girl had wandered off into some tall grasses to pick wildflowers while Harriet and her mother sat in the yard talking.

Suddenly I became aware of something moving toward me thru the grass. So smoothly did it glide and with so little noise. I was frightened! Then reason conquered fear and I knew it was Aunt Harriet, flat on her stomach, and with only the use of her arms and serpentine movement of her body, gliding smoothly along. Mother helped her back to her chair and they laughed. Aunt Harriet then told me that was the way she had gone by many a sentinel during the war.[16]

As the twentieth century began, Harriet Tubman defied the odds. "She would have died long ago," a friend wrote, "but for her indomitable courage and will."[17] Estimates of her age became more exaggerated. By 1911, she was referred to as a "centenarian," but her age at the time was more likely ninety. Harriet Tubman herself was never sure how old she was and put two different birthdates on her pension applications.[18]

At about ninety-two, she sensed her own death. "I am nearing the end of my journey," she told members of the Zion congregation. "I can hear them bells a-ringing, I can hear the angels singing, I can see the hosts a-marching."[19] Visited by a representative of Colored Women's Clubs in New York State, she gave a final message to women's effort to gain the right to vote: "Tell the women to stick together. God is fighting for them and all will be well!"[20]

When she contracted pneumonia, she gathered friends and relatives and led them in singing hymns for her own funeral service. "Swing Low, Sweet Chariot" they sang of the chariot coming to carry Harriet Tubman home. She died a day or so later on March 10, 1913.

A local unit of Civil War veterans fired a volley over her grave. A year later her friend Booker T. Washington, a powerful leader in the movement for education of blacks, delivered a tribute to her at a citywide memorial service as a bronze tablet from the citizens of Auburn was placed on the courthouse:

In Memory of Harriet Tubman . . . Called the "Moses" of her people. . . . With rare courage she led over three hundred Negroes up from slavery to freedom and rendered invaluable service as nurse and spy. . . . She braved every danger and overcame every obstacle. Withal she possessed extraordinary foresight and judgment so that she truthfully said—"On my Underground Railroad I never ran my train off the track and I never lost a passenger."

A NOTE ON RESEARCH

A biographer of Harriet Tubman must sift through 150 years of information, some of it firsthand accounts, some of it recorded history, some of it fiction, much of it legend, none of it in the woman's own hand. We must rely on what others wrote or passed on of what Harriet Tubman said, did, and felt. Separating the fact from the fiction is work for historical detectives.

Her life has most often been told in fiction and fictionalized biography, which includes many fine, dramatic accounts. Two nonfiction biographies provide more reliable information. The first was done in 1868, with a second edition in 1886, by Sarah Bradford from interviews with Harriet Tubman. Bradford said that as far as possible she received corroboration of every incident she included. The second biography, by Earl Conrad, was completed in the late 1930s. Conrad's research was extensive, and I consulted transcripts of his interviews in the Schomburg Collection of the New York Public Library. Another source of primary material is the Blockson Afro-American Collection at Temple University in Philadelphia.

The quotes from Harriet Tubman in this book come from the Bradford and Conrad biographies and from letters Harriet dictated and articles writers published after talking with her.

After reading extensively, I visited Bucktown and traced Harriet Tubman's underground route through Maryland and Delaware as far as the facts and my imagination would allow. I would like to thank the following people for helping me in the research process: Mariline Wilkins, Addie Clash Travers, Monroe William Pinder, Herbert Sherwood, Rev. Edward Jackson, Gloria Henry at the Cambridge Public Library, and Debra Moxey of the Dorchester County Genealogical Magazine; also Charles L. Blockson, James McGowan, William R. Hunn, Mary Howarth, Dr. John Gardner, Priscilla Thompson of the History Store in Wilmington, Del., and Elizabeth Hildebrant and Carolyn Trefts of South Seattle Community College Library.

When the research was completed and the writing begun, Gwen Augustine, Vivian Bowden, Mary O'Brien, Jane Yolen, and Nancy Nordhoff Skinner, of Cottages at Hedgebrook, provided great advice and support.

SOURCE NOTES

Chapter 1

1. George W. Williams, *History of the Negro Race in America,* vol. 2, p. 22.
2. The Pattisons had been given 150 acres of land in the county in 1671. In 1790 the census showed 5,337 slaves in Dorchester County belonging to 274 slaveholding families. Calvin W. Mowbray and Maurice D. Rimpo's "Close-ups of Early Dorchester County History," pp. 40 and 49.
3. Rev. Samuel Miles Hopkins speculated that Harriet Tubman was descended from the Fellatas, also known as the Fula or Fulani. Hopkins was a student of African life and a professor at Auburn Theological Seminary. Harriet Tubman herself relayed the Ashanti comment (Earl Conrad, *Harriet Tubman,* p. 5). It was also commonly agreed that she had not a drop of white blood in her veins.
4. Benjamin Drew, *The Refugee,* p. 20.
5. Sarah Bradford, *Harriet Tubman, The Moses of Her People,* pp. 17–20.
6. Ibid., p. 69.
7. The Brodess family is not well known in Dorchester County today. The last descendant died in 1977. There are several

variations in the spelling of the name: *Brodas, Brodess, Boadas, Brodins.* Sources of information about the Brodesses include bills of sale for some land and for a slave woman and her child, Edward Brodess's will, and Mowbray and Rimpo, *op cit.*

8. Conrad, p. 12.
9. Ibid., p. 9.
10. Charles L. Blockson, *The Underground Railroad,* p. 118.

Chapter 2

1. Jeffrey R. Brackett, *The Negro in Maryland,* p. 101.
2. Williams, *op cit.,* p. 87.
3. Herbert Apthecker, *Nat Turner's Slave Rebellion,* p. 65.
4. Bradford, pp. 109.
5. Ibid., pp. 23–24.
6. Letter dated March 11, 1940, Schomburg Collection.

Chapter 3

1. This assessment of Doc Thompson comes from Ben and Rit who described him to William Still when they escaped from Maryland in 1857 (William Still, *The Underground Railroad,* p. 396). They said Thompson stinted his slaves on food and clothing and "led them a rough life generally." Joseph Brodess died soon after marrying Mary Pattison. She remarried Anthony Thompson, who had two sons, Anthony and Absalom.
2. Samuel Hopkins Adams, "A Slave in the Family," *New Yorker,* p. 36.
3. Frank C. Drake, *New York Herald,* Sept. 11, 1907.
4. Mariline Wilkins, a great-grandniece of Harriet Tubman.
5. Frederick Douglass, *Narrative of the Life of Frederick Douglass,* p. 68.
6. Brackett, p. 55.
7. Ibid., p. 240.
8. *Dictionary of Negro Biography,* p. 606.
9. Bradford, p. 128.

10. Still, p. 395.
11. Blockson, p. 122.
12. Bradford, p. 25.
13. Douglass, p. 117.

Chapter 4

1. Eliza Ann gave supervision of the estate, including the slaves, to an administrator whom she later accused of selling slaves without her knowledge. She did sell a slave woman named Harriet and her child Mary Jane in June 1850. The relationship of this Harriet to Harriet Tubman, if any, is unknown.
2. Bradford, p. 29.
3. Brackett, p. 81.
4. Bradford, p. 29.
5. Conrad, p. 36.
6. Bradford's account of her escape says that Harriet Tubman went on alone the first time when her brothers turned back.
7. Mrs. Helen W. Tatlock of Auburn recounted this story to Earl Conrad.
8. These Friends Meetings have been identified by Priscilla Thompson in an article for *Delaware History,* 1986, 22(1): 1–21.
9. Most of the information about Harriet Tubman's escape comes from what she told to Sarah Bradford, Mrs. Tatlock, and Franklin Sanborn, whose *Commonwealth* article is included in Bradford's book.
10. Bradford, p. 29.
11. Information about the Underground Railroad in Delaware comes from William Still, Priscilla Thompson, and Wilbur H. Siebert, *The Underground Railroad from Slavery to Freedom;* the letters of Thomas Garrett in James A. McGowan, *The Life and Letters of Thomas Garrett;* and Marion Bjornson Reed, "The Underground Railroad and Slavery in Delaware," unpublished master's thesis, University of Delaware. A potentially great source of information was lost when John Hunn ordered his records of the URR burned on his death in 1894.
12. Bradford, p. 30.

129

Chapter 5

1. Charlotte Forten kept a journal from 1854 until 1864, which was edited by Ray Allen Billington and published as *The Journal of Charlotte Forten, A Free Negro in the Slave Era* in 1953 by The Dryden Press, Inc. and in 1961 by Collier Books, London. Forten later met Harriet Tubman when Forten went to teach contrabands on St. Helena Island during the Civil War.
2. Bradford, p. 31.
3. Ibid.
4. Ibid., p. 32.
5. Harkless Bowley gave this account in a letter to Earl Conrad. Bowley was born in Canada in 1853. Some of the details of his story aren't clear, but the main points match other accounts of the rescue.
6. Lerone Bennett, Jr., *Wade in the Water,* pp. 79–94.
7. Bradford, pp. 35–38.
8. Blockson, p. 121.
9. Bradford, p. 38.
10. Douglass writes in *Life and Times of Frederick Douglass,* pp. 329–30 that "on one occasion I had eleven fugitives at the same time under my roof and it was necessary for them to remain with me until I could collect sufficient money to get them to Canada. It was the largest number I ever had at any one time, and I had some difficulty in providing so many with food and shelter, but, as may well be imagined, they were not very fastidious in either direction, and were well content with very plain food, and a strip of carpet on the floor for a bed, or a place on the straw in the barnloft."

Chapter 6

1. Still's father freed himself through self-purchase. His mother made one unsuccessful attempt to escape and then ran away with two of her four children. William was born in the North, in 1821, the youngest of their eighteen children. He left the family farm in New Jersey at age twenty, moved to Philadelphia, and taught himself to read and write. He

started as a janitor and mail clerk for the Pennsylvania Society for Promoting the Abolition of Slavery and worked his way into greater responsibility.

2. Still recorded six of Harriet's groups and mentioned others who were inspired by her to escape. His first entry mentioning her was dated December 28, 1854.

3. Railroads were not known in the United States until about 1850, so the first term used was probably *underground road*. The underground passage quote has been attributed to John Calhoun (Hildegarde H. Swift, *Railroad to Freedom*, p. 96).

4. Still, p. 74.

5. Earl Conrad, *Harriet Tubman, Negro Soldier and Abolitionist*, p. 12.

6. Siebert, p. 118.

7. Reed, no page number.

8. Bradford, pp. 53–55.

9. Thomas Garrett's letters, which describe several of Harriet's journeys, have been collected by James A. McGowan in *The Life and Letters of Thomas Garrett, Station Master on the Underground Railroad,* Moylan, Pa.: The Whimsie Press, 1977. Garrett had been a member of the Friends Meeting in Wilmington, but he left to join the Longwood Meeting in Chester County, which was formed in 1853 by Friends who had been disowned by their own meetings for their radical stands against slavery. Garrett was in constant touch with members of the meeting concerning passengers on the underground. By the time of the Civil War, Garrett said he had helped more than 2,700 fugitives.

10. McGowan, p. 135.

11. Bradford, p. 63.

12. We do not know if Henry's wife was ever freed. Harriet made several attempts to free a "sister" in the late 1850s but was unsuccessful. The sister could have been a sister-in-law.

13. Bradford, p. 71.

14. Still, p. 298.

15. William Wells Brown, *The Rising Son*, p. 538.

16. Rosa Belle Holt, "A Heroine in Ebony," *Chautauquan*, p. 461.

Chapter 7

1. The story of Joe's escape is recounted in Bradford, pp. 39–48 and confirmed by Thomas Garrett's letters (McGowan, p. 136) and William Still's records.
2. McGowan, p. 136.
3. This bridge crossing story was recounted by several writers, but not all agreed as to which group was involved. Thompson puts Harriet's brothers hiding under the straw in the December 1854 rescue. Bradford identifies it as Joe's group.
4. Conrad, *Harriet Tubman,* p. 83 and Langston Hughes, *Famous Negro Heroes of America,* p. 110.
5. Conrad, p. 102.
6. Reed.
7. The average reward for returning a fugitive in Maryland was approaching $200, $500 if the slave was returned from Pennsylvania (Thompson, p. 53). Doc Thompson made the statement that Minty was worth only $200 to $250 in a chancery case heard in 1853 (Mowbray, p. 57).
8. This story was told in several sources: Bradford, p. 34; Thomas Higginson as quoted in Bennett, *Pioneers in Protest,* p. 138; Drake, *New York Herald;* Thomas Garrett (McGowan, p. 125), and Wyman, Lillie B. Chace, "Harriet Tubman," *New England Magazine,* March 1896, vol. 14, p. 110–18.
9. Bradford, pp. 73–75, letter from Garrett.
10. Conrad, pp. 93–94; McGowan, pp. 139–43; Still, p. 249.
11. Still, pp. 248–50.
12. Maryland passed a law in 1841 setting this penalty for any free colored person who received through the mail or had in his possession any abolition handbill, pamphlet, newspaper, pictorial representation, etc. Green served five years and then was pardoned by the governor of Maryland in 1862 on condition of his leaving the state (Brackett, p. 225).
13. Conrad, p. 94.
14. Ibid., p. 97.
15. Blockson, p. 174.

Chapter 8

1. James and his family and Mary Ann and her family were both living in the same house in Chatham. William and

Catherine were in St. Catharines as were Harriet Tubman's parents. Brothers John Henry, Benjamin, Robert, and Henry were also in Canada. They took the last name Stewart in freedom, possibly after John Stewart, the shipbuilder in Dorchester County.

2. Alice Brickler recounted this story in letters to Earl Conrad. Margaret Stewart grew up in Auburn, married, had three children, including Alice, and died about 1930. Margaret was said to exactly resemble Harriet.

3. James B. Clarke, "An Hour with Harriet Tubman," unnumbered pages.

4. Brown led a raid into Missouri which freed a number of slaves but resulted in the death of one slaveholder. At Pottawatomie, in May 1856, his small band murdered five proslavery men.

5. The other two were Samuel Gridley Howe, a Boston philanthropist, and George L. Stearns, a businessman.

6. Conrad, p. 115.

7. Franklin Sanborn, *The Life and Letters of John Brown,* p. 452.

8. Bradford, p. 118.

9. Truman Nelson, *The Old Man, John Brown at Harpers Ferry,* p. 24.

10. Mariline Wilkins.

11. Conrad, p. 120.

12. Ibid., p. 105.

13. Brown, p. 536.

14. Conrad, pp. 108–9.

15. Ibid., p. 110.

Chapter 9

1. Bennett, p. 141.

2. The brother who came to claim Nalle probably had the same father and a white mother. Whatever the color of his skin, Nalle was a slave because he was born to a slave. Slave women had little power to resist the sexual advances of their masters. Such tangled parentage was not uncommon.

3. Conrad, p. 134.

4. Bradford, pp. 119–128 and Philip Sterling, *Four Took Freedom,* pp. 21–22.

5. "The Fugitive Slave Law and Its Victims," 1861, quoted in Conrad, p. 234. There were other famous rescues and attempted rescues in the years of the Fugitive Slave Law. Joshua Glover was forcibly rescued from a courthouse in Milwaukee in 1854. Thomas Sims was captured in Boston in 1851, tried and returned to slavery in Georgia where he died. Anthony Burns was the last fugitive slave returned to Virginia from Boston, after a hearing that provoked angry opposition from abolitionists in 1854. Burns was later purchased out of slavery by Northern friends, but he was in ill health and did not live long. (See Virginia Hamilton, *Anthony Burns: The Defeat and Triumph of a Fugitive Slave.*)

6. Earl Conrad, *The Governor and His Lady*, p. 320.

7. Conrad, p. 140.

8. *Liberator*, June 1, 1860.

9. Conrad, p. 100.

10. Thompson, p. 19.

11. Still, p. 531.

12. Conrad, p. 143.

Chapter 10

1. Drew, p. 10

2. Bradford, p. 92. The Emancipation Proclamation freeing the slaves under Union control was issued on January 1, 1863.

3. Sanborn, p. 500.

4. Conrad, p. 36. The Sea Island Negroes spoke the Gullah dialect.

5. Ibid.

6. Helen Beal Woodward, *The Bold Women*, p. 238.

7. Mariline Wilkins.

8. Some slaves had worked on steamers in the interisland and local coastal trade. One, Robert Smalls, was a wheelsman on a steamer called *Planter* and was so trusted by the captain he had almost become a pilot. He and friends seized the *Planter* from Charleston Harbor in May 1862 and delivered it and themselves to freedom behind federal lines. He was put to work for the Union. The pilots Harriet Tubman recruited were Charles Simmons and Samuel Hayward.

9. Conrad, p. 168.

10. Brown, p. 538.
11. Capt. John F. Lay, Confederate investigating officer, *Official History of the War of Rebellion* (Conrad, p. 171).
12. Conrad, p. 174.
13. Conrad, p. 169.
14. Letter to Sanborn, June 30, 1863 (Conrad, p. 177). Bloomers took their name from Amelia Bloomer, a temperance journal editor in Seneca Falls, New York, who maintained that women have the right to control their own wardrobe, even if it meant wearing the pantaloons some people were advocating in the 1850s.
15. Conrad, *Negro Soldier*, p. 40.

Chapter 11

1. Letter to Sanborn, op. cit.
2. Holt, p. 462.
3. Eugene D. Genovese, *Roll, Jordan Roll*, p. 142. Child made these comments in a letter to John Greenleaf Whittier on Jan. 21, 1862.
4. *Narrative of Sojourner Truth*, p. 174.
5. Conrad, *Harriet Tubman*, p. 162.
6. Cranesbill was used by Native Americans as a treatment for dysentery. The roots of the white pond lily are listed as a treatment for dysentery in *A Modern Herbal*, Mrs. M. Grieve, 1971.
7. Conrad, p. 163.
8. Conrad, "The Charles P. Wood Manuscripts of Harriet Tubman," p. 93.

Chapter 12

1. Accounts of the murder and trial appeared in the *Baltimore American* on October 7, 1867, and the *Baltimore Sun,* Dec. 17, 1867.
2. Conversation with Frank C. Drake (Bennett, p. 144).
3. Eva was the granddaughter of Harriet's brother James Isaac, who had taken the last name *Stewart*. Eva was born in St. Catharines, but after her mother and then her father died when she was eleven or twelve, she came to live with Har-

riet. Eva Stewart Northup's daughter is Mariline Wilkins, who now lives in Philadelphia.

4. Bradford, p. 9.
5. Holt, p. 461.
6. Conrad, p. 181.
7. Clarke, unnumbered.
8. Bradford, p. 135.
9. Ibid., p. 5.
10. Holt, p. 461.
11. Adams, p. 33.
12. Conrad, p. 210.
13. Clarke.
14. Ibid.
15. Conrad, p. 220.
16. Brickler letters.
17. Wyman, p. 118.
18. Harkless Bowley wrote to Earl Conrad that "none of [the] old people of our family knew their correct ages. I got my father's age from an old white man who said he and my father was boys together. . . ." Harriet Tubman's birthdate has been estimated as from 1810 to 1825. Even she didn't know for sure, as Frederick Douglass explained: "By far the larger part of the slaves know as little of their age as horses know of theirs. I do not remember to have ever met a slave who could tell of his birthday. They seldom come nearer to it than planting time, harvest-time, cherry-time, spring-time or fall-time."
19. Bennett, *Wade,* p. 94.
20. Hallie Q. Brown, *Homespun Heroines,* p. 65.

FOR FURTHER READING

Bennett, Lerone, Jr. *Wade in the Water, Great Moments in Black History.* Chicago: Johnson Publishing Co., 1979.

Blockson, Charles L. *The Underground Railroad: First Person Narratives of Escape to Freedom in the North.* New York: Prentice-Hall Press, 1987.

Bradford, Sarah H. *Harriet Tubman, the Moses of Her People.* Gloucester, Mass., Peter Smith, 1981.

Conrad, Earl. *Harriet Tubman.* New York: Paul S. Erikkson, Inc., 1969.

Douglass, Frederick. *The Life and Times of Frederick Douglass.* New York: Thomas Y. Crowell, 1966.

Hamilton, Virginia. *Anthony Burns: The Defeat and Triumph of a Fugitive Slave.* New York: Alfred A. Knopf, 1988.

Lester, Julius. *To Be a Slave.* New York: Scholastic, 1968.

Petry, Ann. *Harriet Tubman, Conductor on the Underground Railroad.* New York: Pocket Books, 1971.

Sterling, Philip. *Four Took Freedom: The Lives of Harriet Tubman, Robert Smalls, Frederick Douglass, and Blance K. Bruce.* New York: Doubleday, 1967.

Swift, Hildegarde H. *The Railroad to Freedom.* New York: Harcourt Brace, 1932.

BIBLIOGRAPHY

Adams, Samuel Hopkins. "A Slave in the Family," *New Yorker.* Dec. 13, 1947.

Apthecker, Herbert. *Nat Turner's Slave Rebellion.* New York: Humanities Press, 1966.

Bennett, Lerone, Jr. *Pioneers in Protest.* Baltimore, Md.: Penguin Books, Inc., 1968.

———. *Wade in the Water, Great Moments in Black History,* Chicago: Johnson Publishing Co., 1979.

Blockson, Charles L. *The Underground Railroad: First-Person Narratives of Escapes to Freedom in the North.* New York: Prentice Hall Press, 1987.

Brackett, Jeffrey R. *The Negro in Maryland.* Baltimore, 1889. Johns Hopkins University studies in historical and political science, extra volume VI. Freeport, 1969.

Bradford, Sarah H. *Harriet Tubman, The Moses of Her People.* Lockwood & Son, 1886. Gloucester, Mass.: Peter Smith, 1981.

Brown, Hallie Q., *Homespun Heroines and Other Women of Distinction.* Zenia, Oh: Aldine Pub. Co., 1926. New York: Oxford University Press, 1988.

Brown, William Wells. *The Rising Son.* New York: Negro Universities Press, 1970. Boston: A. G. Brown & Co., 1874.

Clarke, James B. "An Hour with Harriet Tubman," Los Angeles: Grafton Publishing Co., 1911.

Conrad, Earl. *The Governor and His Lady*. New York: G. P. Putnam's Sons, 1960.

————. *Harriet Tubman*. New York: Paul S. Erikkson, 1969.

————. *Harriet Tubman, Negro Soldier and Abolitionist*. International Publishers, 1942.

Douglass, Frederick. *The Life and Times of Frederick Douglass*. Boston: DeWolfe, Fiske & Co., 1892. New York: Thomas Y. Crowell, 1966.

————. *Narrative of the Life of Frederick Douglass, An American Slave*. Cambridge, Mass.: Belknap Press, 1960. (first published in 1845).

Drew, Benjamin. *The Refugee*. Boston: John P. Jewett & Co., 1856; New York: Negro Universities Press, 1968.

Genovese, Eugene D. *Roll, Jordan, Roll: The World the Slaves Made*. New York: Vintage Books, Random House, 1972.

Hamilton, Virginia. *Anthony Burns: The Defeat and Triumph of a Fugitive Slave*. New York: Alfred A. Knopf, 1988.

Holt, Rosa Belle. "A Heroine in Ebony," *Chautauquan*, July, 1896. Vol. 23:4, pp. 459–62.

Hughes, Langston. *Famous Negro Heroes of America*. New York: Dodd, Mead, 1958.

The Journal of Charlotte L. Forten. Edited by Ray Allen Billington. London: Collier Books, 1961.

McGowan, James A. *The Life and Letters of Thomas Garrett, Station Master on the Underground Railroad*. Moylan, Pa.: The Whimsie Press, 1977.

Mowbray, Calvin W. and Rimpo, Maurice D. "Close-ups of Early Dorchester County History," 2nd ed., Silver Spring, Md.: Family Line Publications, 1988.

Narrative of Sojourner Truth. New York: Arno Press and the New York Times, 1968.

Nelson, Truman. *The Old Man, John Brown at Harpers Ferry*. New York: Holt, Rinehart, & Winston, 1973.

Reed, Marion Bjornson. "The Underground Railroad and Slavery in Delaware," unpublished master's thesis, University of Delaware, Newark, Del., 1928.

Sanborn, Franklin B. *The Life and Letters of John Brown*. Boston: Roberts, 1891.

139

Siebert, Wilbur H. *The Underground Railroad from Slavery to Freedom.* Gloucester, Mass.: Peter Smith, 1968. First published 1898.

Sterling, Philip. *Four Took Freedom.* New York: Doubleday, 1967.

Still, William. *The Underground Railroad.* New York: Arno Press and the New York Times, 1968. First published in 1873.

Swift, Hildegarde H. *The Railroad to Freedom.* New York: Harcourt Brace, 1932.

Thompson, Priscilla, "Harriet Tubman, Thomas Garrett, and the Underground Railroad," *Delaware History,* 1986, 22 (1): 1–21.

Williams, George W. *History of the Negro Race in America, 1619–1880.* Arno Press and the New York Times, 1968. First published 1883.

Woodward, Helen Beal. *The Bold Women.* New York: Farrar, Straus, & Young, 1953.

Wyman, Lillie B. Chace, "Harriet Tubman," *New England Magazine.* March, 1896, vol. 14:110–18.

INDEX

ABOUT THE AUTHOR

Judith Bentley is a teacher and writer. In the process of researching this book she traveled to Harriet Tubman's home in Bucktown, Maryland, and met with Tubman's descendants in Maryland and Pennsylvania. Ms. Bentley lives with her husband in Washington State.